SEND MY ROOTS RAIN

SEND MY ROOTS RAIN

Refreshing the Spiritual Life of Priests

Christopher Chapman

CANTERBURY
PRESS

Norwich

© Christopher Chapman 2019

First published in 2019 by the Canterbury Press Norwich
Editorial office
3rd Floor, Invicta House
108–114 Golden Lane
London EC1Y 0TG, UK
www.canterburypress.co.uk

Canterbury Press is an imprint of Hymns Ancient & Modern Ltd
(a registered charity)
Hymns Ancient & Modern® is a registered trademark of
Hymns Ancient & Modern Ltd
13a Hellesdon Park Road
Norwich
Norfolk NR6 5DR, UK

Scripture quotations are from New Revised Standard Version Bible: Anglicized
Edition, copyright © 1989, 1995 National Council of the Churches of Christ in the
United States of America. Used by permission. All rights reserved worldwide.

British Library Cataloguing in Publication data
A catalogue record for this book is available
from the British Library

978 1 78622 219 0

Typeset by Mary Matthews

Printed and bound in Great Britain by
CPI Group (UK) Ltd

For Tony, Peter, Robin, Doug, Greg,
Alistair and Brian

Contents

Acknowledgements

I am grateful to Christine Smith and all at Canterbury Press for their openness to what I proposed and for their continued support.

This book rests on the experiences and insights of many priests. Some I consulted with during the early days of forming my ideas and putting them into words. Their thoughts helped to broaden the horizons of my writing. Others generously set aside time to read the text and give helpful feedback. Over the years I have listened to priests in the context of spiritual direction and retreat work; their hard-won insights helped to form the understanding of priesthood I put forward here. Still more priests have been my teachers, mentors, colleagues and friends. The views expressed in this book are my own; and they are also the fruit of this lifelong dialogue. I do not name names for fear of leaving people out, but I am grateful for what you have given me.

I am thankful for the support of friends, not least those in my book group, whose encouragement helped me stay with the task through the times when it became more challenging. Finally, though her visible footfall through these pages is small, I owe much to June, my wife, who continues to help me be a better human being, and has to put up with the days when that's not quite working!

Preface

Alleluia! Amen

I was ordained in a sports hall, wearing appropriate soft-soled shoes so as not to mark the floor. The parish church was deemed too small to host the occasion, so instead of playing badminton or five-a-side football I came along to have my life changed. The local paper covered the unusual event: 'More than 900 Roman Catholics joined in a service marking the ordination of 26-year-old Christopher Chapman of Victoria Road, Ashford, who became the first Ashford man ordained into the Catholic Church since the Reformation.' The parish newsletter of the following week included a quote attributed to Cardinal Manning on the priesthood:

> The end of man is the glory of God. The end of a Christian is the greater glory of God. The end of a priest is the greatest glory of God.

No pressure there then! One picture of the day shows me blessing my sister. The next shows the two of us looking at each other in amazement as if to say, 'How did this happen? What are all these people doing here?'

I received many cards and gifts on that day. The one that meant most to me had just two words: 'Alleluia! Amen.' The 'alleluia' expressed my heartfelt sense of gratitude for the way God had gone with me on my journey thus far. The 'amen' acknowledged the struggle it had involved and my awareness that, for all the momentous nature of the ordination ceremony, I was still the all-too-human 'Chris'. I was putting my trust in God's faith in me.

Each priest holds together their humanity with the received expectations of the role they say their 'amen' to. No formational programme can adequately prepare priests for the ministry that lies ahead. Beyond ordination day, priests still need the laying on of many hands in support, encouragement and kindness. Above all, priests need the continual refreshment that is the gift of the Spirit of God. My hope and prayer in writing is that among these words there will be rain for the roots of your being.

Easter 2019

1

One Who is Like His Brothers and Sisters in Every Respect

The Word is made flesh

> He had to become like his brothers and sisters in every respect, so that he might be a merciful and faithful high priest in the service of God … Because he himself was tested by what he suffered, he is able to help those who are being tested.[1]

In time, and beyond time, God is expressed by incarnation. Wherever we are, and whoever we are, God is alongside and within us. God's choice – always and for all – is to feel all pain, share all joy and be inside all struggle. It is this mystery that priests of our time are closest to. Through their voices the words of Jesus in the Gospel are spoken afresh; their hands take and bless the bread of our life and the cup of our salvation. Their ministry celebrates the beginnings and endings of our earthly existence. The rhythm of worship they maintain holds us in awareness of moments and seasons hallowed through God's movement through them. In the community and care they seek to build, the Word is made flesh and lives among us.

In sharing Jesus' cup, priests also taste his struggles. How could it not be so? For the one they serve laughs and cries, rages and rejoices in all our varied faces. Sometimes it hurts to be human, and priests must go there too – not just in the suffering of other people, but in meeting the frailties of their own humanity. Every priest must carry the burdens and gifts of their history and personality; each has to work with the uneasy blend of their strengths and weaknesses. Yet these difficult truths are also the graced places of God's indwelling.

For the most part priests are generous and faithful people who

---

[1] Hebrews 2.17–18.

have thrown themselves into meeting the needs of the individuals and communities they serve; sometimes they do not know when or how to stop. Expectations can weigh heavily – not least those that priests have of themselves. In the attempt to reflect the reality of God, priests can become caught in webs of perfectionism that bear no relation to who they are. The vision of the incarnation that underpins this ministry becomes mislaid when priests believe they can only express God by leaving aside their particular humanity.

For all that a priest dons clothes that suggest their difference from those they minister to, they are of one flesh. Before anything else, a priest is a disciple in need of teaching, forming, restoring, loving and belonging. God does not love everyone, but each one. Priests, who spend their lives seeking to lead others into awareness of the presence and activity of God, are challenged to let Christ take them aside, away from the crowd. *Send My Roots Rain* explores what might happen within this encounter and the need every priest has of it.

A spiritual house and a holy priesthood

> Come to him, a living stone, though rejected by mortals yet chosen and precious in God's sight, and like living stones, let yourselves be built into a spiritual house, to be a holy priesthood, to offer spiritual sacrifices acceptable to God through Jesus Christ … You are a chosen race, a royal priesthood, a holy nation, God's own people, in order that you may proclaim the mighty acts of him who called you out of darkness into his marvellous light.
>
> Once you were not a people, but now you are God's people; once you had not received mercy, but now you have received mercy.[2]

For the author of the letter of Peter, the destiny of the people formed in Jesus Christ is to be a holy priesthood, chosen and consecrated for the work of God's mercy. As this people grew in number and diversity they established an order of priests to help express their identity and mission, and to nurture their common life. Peter's words remind all Christians of who they are and the task they share. For those who are ordained priests these words become a summons. You

---

[2] 1 Peter 2.4–10.

– as a priest – are to allow God's hands to build you. You are a living stone, purposefully chosen, to be formed into a spiritual house. You who have received being, belonging and mercy are to draw all who are lost into the wonder of their being and belonging through the mercy of God. You are to name and proclaim the Christ who called you out of darkness into marvellous light. You are to make your life a thanksgiving offering, a sacrifice of praise, in response to the abundance of God's giving.

Can you do that? Can you be that? The mystery the words attempt to describe is overwhelming. And yet Peter's words also give their hearers a way into the mystery. Though you reject yourself as too small, God chooses you to be a living stone. You cannot create this life yourself; it is God who will form you into a spiritual house if you go on allowing this to happen. You must receive mercy if you are to share mercy. If you welcome God into your darkness then light will flow from your life. This is the work of God and humanity working together, never apart. The 'holy priesthood' is inseparable from the 'spiritual house'. This beautiful but challenging vision of what it is to be a priest only makes sense through the very first words: 'Come to him'.

In the midst of the very real demands of ministry it is easy to lose one's place: the vision fades and the pressure builds. In a difficult moment – or after years of erosion – a priest might wonder, 'Am I a living stone or a forgotten and useless rock, kicked about by those who pass by?' Even so, the hand of the one who knows and values the form and texture of each individual stone is never far away. 'Let yourselves be built,' Peter implores. The formation of a spiritual house is both possible and practical, whatever our personality or context.

The tree by the waterside

> Happy are those … [whose] delight is in the law of the Lord,
> and on his law they meditate day and night.
> They are like trees planted by streams of water,
> which yield their fruit in its season,
> and their leaves do not wither.[3]

---

[3] Psalm 1.1–3.

The book of Psalms begins with a picture of a spreading tree, green of leaf and bearing bountiful fruit, year after year. Unstated, yet understood, the psalmist knows the importance of roots. The visible top growth that draws the eye rests on the unseen movement downwards to where the water flows. Recently I walked by a canal in Yorkshire. It was a calm day with bright sun. The tall branches reaching up to the sky were reflected back down into the water. This was no illusion: the depth and breadth of the hidden roots of a tree must match that of its top growth, or the whole will fail. Roots provide stability, so that outward growth is held secure. And season by season, roots draw up nutrients for life and water that saves them from withering.

Life as a priest is challenging. It can be deeply rewarding and demanding in equal measure. Priests have high expectations of themselves in terms of competence, availability and problem solving. The ministry of a priest is endlessly diverse; the job description can become a runaway, eluding all bounds. Ready or not, many priests find themselves drawn into roles not anticipated within their ordination service, becoming 'learn-as-you-go' caretakers, counsellors, managers, recruiters, accountants and jugglers. This many-branched life depends on generous roots. In the pages that follow I set out to explore attitudes, practices and forms of spiritual life capable of continuing to motivate, sustain and give meaning to the earthy reality of ministry shaped by meetings, services, emails, doorbells, and encounters with a kaleidoscope of people.

Where and when do these roots of ministry begin to form? Perhaps they begin their downward quest from experience of the goodness of God. Or perhaps a person is moved by human need and senses God's invitation to respond to it. Or they see in this way of life some answer to the puzzle of who they are and what they desire to live for. These roots enable the initial testing of vocation. Selectors will probe to explore how well founded this movement towards ordination is. But the roots have to go on deepening through long years of service. The vital questions never go away: 'Who are you, God, and who am I in you? How do I go on drawing life from you? How are you at work in my life, and what are you drawing me to be or to do?'

While people of all faiths and none now speak of the spiritual dimension of life, from a Christian perspective spirituality concerns life in the Holy Spirit. Here is the living water of rain and river: the source of all being and becoming. 'Spiritual life' is not some rarefied higher plane of existence removed from the realities of daily commitments and relationships; it is every atom and moment of living, experienced in the Spirit. Here is where ministry is rooted. Life as a priest is complex, yet at its heart are simple truths: priests seek to remain open to God in the service of other people; priests share all human longings, needs and desires. How then can priests remain responsive to the Spirit within the recurring opportunities, tasks and pressures inherent within the patterns of their lives? How do they avoid becoming completely consumed by these pressures? Where can they find living water to refresh their relationships and ministry?

Tall branches must draw life from deep roots.

The shape of this book

The Word is made flesh within the realities of our experience. I will begin by exploring the context within which priesthood is practised today and in particular the pressures that stem from the expectations people typically have of priests, or priests have of themselves. How is a priest to respond to these expectations? To what degree do they serve or hinder responsiveness to the Spirit?

We are living stones designed to be formed into a spiritual house. How do priests understand their identity? I will examine some underlying questions about what it is to be a priest:

- Is a priest another order of human being by virtue of their ordination?
- To what extent can priesthood express personal identity?
- Do priests belong in the spiritual arrivals lounge, or do they remain spiritual travellers?
- Do priests have a distinctive spirituality, or do they share a common human path expressed within a particular context?
- What image or understanding of God do priests express or respond to through their attitudes and actions?

While there will often be more than one way of answering these questions, the stances assumed in relation to them will shape the way priesthood is lived and experienced.

Like a tree by the waterside, the leaves and fruits of ministry depend on the nutrients drawn up by deep roots. What forms of spiritual life are capable of sustaining and enriching the work of a priest, while meeting the realities of priestly ministry? It is perhaps inevitable that there is no 'one size fits all' pattern capable of encompassing every expression of priestly character and ministry. Contexts, personal histories, inherited traditions of worship and personalities are as varied as can be. And yet there are common orientations and attitudes that go with the life of a priest as expressed within rites of ordination. These orientations and stances open the way for listening and responding to the Spirit within – rather than despite – the day to day experience of being a priest. As I explore this common ground I will also outline practical steps that priests might take to guard and nurture their life in the Spirit. There are many ways to pray and a variety of means of being with God in the midst of activity.

I will begin by considering Jesus' call to his disciples to 'be with him'. They were to learn and grow from remaining by his side. Priestly ministry flows from, and returns to, this intimate companionship. Here is the home where we always belong. In prayer we draw life from mutual abiding: we are in God, and God is in us.

A priest breaks open and shares the word of God. Where is this word to be found? We ponder it in Scripture and we receive it in daily life. Jesus urged his followers to look and to listen, to be attentive and to watch. The world is full of parables for those willing to take notice. Given the demands of ministry, how does a priest make room to receive the word that is always being sown? Amid activity, we are invited to become contemplatives. The muddle of experience can become a place of encounter and revelation.

Though priests represent the institution of the Church, they are also pilgrim travellers. The call to follow Jesus provides orientation for their journey. The faith they seek to build up in others is not the illusion of immovable certainty, but vulnerable trust in one who draws us on, step by step, to a destination that remains unseen. Priests need tools for discernment to be able to recognize the invitation of the Spirit. Where does the path of life go? What is it God is bringing about in me and in those I serve? How can I step out in cooperation with this movement?

A priest has authority and is also a servant. There is power attached to ministry. Rather than misuse it, or back away from its reality, how do priests own and use it for good? Humility is one fruit of prayerful self-examination. Under the gaze of God we grow into truth that sets us free to give the best of ourselves, without the need to apologize for who we are or anxiously shore up our sense of worth.

The Eucharist celebrates our communion with one another in God. Priests are cast in the role of givers; but the inner life of God requires all to become receivers too. How do priests allow God – and other people – to provide them with the food they need? Where community is lacking they might need to actively seek it. What forms of common life are open to priests?

The sacraments and the symbolic language of worship express how God is met within the physicality of our experience. We are – together – the Body of Christ and we remind one another of this every time we celebrate the Eucharist. How do priests honour their own bodily being? How do they pray with the body rather than despite it?

Priests are heralds of the good news of the love of God expressed through the life, death and resurrection of Jesus Christ. A gospel continues to be written within their lives. How does the Jesus story interweave with their experience, past and present? What particular hope and joy is given to them, first to be refreshed by, and then to share?

Through their personal care and the structures they help put in place to serve people's needs, priests seek to provide safe refuges for vulnerable people. But priests also need their own places of shelter. Aelred of Rievaulx believed that friendship was a beautiful expression of the love of God. What part does friendship play within the life and prayer of a priest? Ministry makes us all too aware of people, places and the passing of time, but what are the possibilities of finding shelter within them?

A priest is a minister of reconciliation and forgiveness. They seek to bring healing amid hurt and brokenness; but what of priests themselves? Ordination provides no immunity from human weakness; if anything its demands expose more immediately whatever flaws we carry. Moving away from the notion of a priest as a reflection of the perfection of Christ, I believe it is more helpful for a priest to model what it is to be a human being open to God, through the grace of Christ and the communion of the Spirit. Jesus greeted the disciples in the locked room with peace. The conversational prayer of 'colloquy' is one way we can begin to receive the healing and wholeness he intends for us.

Having outlined these ways in which rain might reach down to roots, I will go on to explore whether adopting a personal 'rule' or 'way' of life might prove a practical means of ensuring rain regularly brings refreshment to a priest's spiritual life. In this context, a rule of life is chosen rather than imposed, individually shaped rather than of universal form, and will continue to evolve rather than be set in stone. I will set out a framework which may prove useful in forming and reviewing a rule of life that has the right blend of achievability and challenge.

Finally, I will suggest some ways in which the wider Church might nurture the spiritual life of priests. Dioceses and local congregations have a duty of care. Processes aimed at the initial and ongoing formation of priests must give room for deep roots in God to be developed and sustained. Every priest has to personally appropriate what they need to continue being refreshed by the Spirit; but external support and encouragement are also vital.

Though my reflections will largely draw on the experience of Anglican and Roman Catholic priests, I hope that much of what I write will be applicable to ministers from other traditions. The Spirit willingly crosses our human boundaries. While in writing I have in mind priests themselves, and those preparing for ordination, I hope these words will also be helpful to those who contribute to the formation of priests and all those who wonder how best they can understand and support the ministry of their own parish clergy.

Experiencing priesthood

Through the writing of this book I have come to realize just how long I have been pondering what it means to be a priest. The idea of becoming a Catholic priest was around for me before I left primary school. The idea solidified into what I recognized as a call while I was at university. I was ordained in 1982. I left the priesthood – after much agonizing – after nine years in parish ministry. I had no idea what happened next. Priesthood had become the totality of my existence and I struggled to imagine what could possibly follow. After a number of unsuccessful job applications, I was accepted for a post with the Anglican Diocese of Southwark developing ministry within inner-city areas and outer estates. Over the course of the next 24 years my role evolved to include parish development, theological education, pastoral care training and spiritual formation. Inevitably people asked me why I did not go on to apply for ordained ministry within the Church of England. But for all my profound respect for expressions of priestly ministry within the Anglican tradition, I sensed that the Catholic Church remained integral to my story. I also recognized that I carried with me unresolved questions about what it meant to be a priest, and how this related to my own experience. Such deep questions are unsettling, and yet if we stay with them there is much to be received. I hope this book carries some of the fruit of that reflection.

The work in Southwark gave me fresh opportunities to be alongside priests from a different tradition from my own. For many of them, the coming of an outsider provided opportunities to share not only their joys and successes, but also their frustrations and weariness. Perhaps because they knew I had been a priest – and yet came from a different 'tribe' – they judged it safe to say how it really was. I often came away moved by the depth of their commitment and the resourcefulness of their ministry, but also with a sense of their isolation and struggle.

For many years I have been privileged to accompany priests from different traditions and contexts through spiritual direction and retreats. It is a large part of my work today. Here priests are able – literally or metaphorically – to take off their dog collars and get in touch with themselves afresh as people and as disciples. God is interested in their work; but also interested in them.

In accompanying priests – and now in writing about them – I recognize there are so many experiences that I have not had. I do not know from the inside what it is to be a priest for 30 or 40 years. I do not know what pressures come from being a woman and a priest, or what it is like to be told that your sexual orientation is at odds with the teaching of the Church. However, there is an upside for this task of writing about the spiritual life of priests in the way my own story has unfolded. Those nine years of parish ministry – and the formation that preceded them – have given me a foothold in understanding life as a priest. I can get in touch with what it was like to be within; and I can also stand outside. I can look at priests as human beings as well as ministers of the Church. Experience has helped me to take seriously the work of a priest while not losing sight of the person who undertakes this work.

In the course of writing this book I have sought out wider experiences and insights than my own from a range of people who accepted the call to priesthood. I do not set out to offer a last word on how priestly spirituality is expressed. I hope – with the help of all those who have generously shared their own experiences – that I can at least share *a* word. I give it with gratitude for all those priests who helped me into a living faith and continue to offer me their friendship and support. I offer these words with deep respect and with love.

Send my roots rain

Mine, O thou lord of life, send my roots rain.[4]

It often seems that the deepest of prayers have the fewest words. This prayer comes at the end of a poem composed by the priest Gerard Manley Hopkins in March 1889. Since ordination he had been moved from parish to parish, encountering experiences of human hardship his upbringing had not prepared him for. At the time of writing he was struggling with a teaching post in Dublin, a long way from his home. In the poem he describes signs of the year's regeneration and of the stirring of new life. Birds were building their nests; the once bare ground was crowded with fresh green shoots. But spring had not yet come to his life. Haunted by recurring bouts of depression,

---

[4] 'Thou art indeed just, Lord, if I contend with thee', in *The Poems of Gerard Manley Hopkins*, 4th edn, revised and enlarged, 1967, edited by W. H. Gardner and N. H. MacKenzie, Oxford: Oxford University Press.

and feeling far from the people and places he loved, he found himself unable to 'breed one work that wakes'. And why was this? Why did God withhold favour when he had dedicated his life in God's service? His prayer was a cry of the heart: 'send my roots rain'.

Priests are not immune from sensing their land is dry; there may be days, months or years when no spring of living water rises to bring life to their weary spirits. Like Hopkins, their work continues faithfully, and those on the outside may not detect the pain within. On the whole priests are practised in perseverance, whatever is going on within. 'The show must go on'; there are always people waiting for what they offer.

It isn't always like this. Being a priest, alongside people at key transitional points of life, is often deeply rewarding and humbling. There are opportunities to make a real difference to the lives of individuals and communities. The very nature of the role, centred on the living word of Scripture and the eucharistic table, can bring an intense awareness of the presence and goodness of God. And living on the edge of life and death – as priests must do – there is laughter too. It seems to be a rule that the more serious the setting, the more explosive is the potential for humour. But the pressure of expectations people have of priests and priests have of themselves is great, and sometimes the burden is heavy.

Nor are priests protected from the ordinary challenges of being human. For all have a story, and all have their wounds. We carry within us the desire to be loved and valued for who we are. We want to feel useful; we hope to make a mark. We sometimes find relationships disturbing and mystifying. There are days when we look in the mirror and don't like what we see. We get things right and we muck things up. We sometimes become sick in body or mind. We have all found a way to present ourselves to the world that isn't 'the whole truth and nothing but the truth'. We are still in there searching for a way to be 'me', without knowing who this 'me' really is. And yet, as uncomfortable as this struggle with the vulnerability of being human can be, it is the ground of priestly ministry. For before anything else, priests must know their need of God. Life flows from continuing to allow the compassion of God to seep into, and then overflow, their weakness.

It is not an easy time to be a priest – if there ever was one. Is a priest respected, or suspected, in a time when sexual abuse cases are never far from the headlines? From representing the mainstream of religious affiliation, now priests represent one more minority interest. Even among those searching for meaning and for God, a representative of a religious institution may be seen as more of a barrier than a gateway. We are familiar with one of the catchphrases of our time: 'I'm spiritual but I'm not religious.' So why look for answers from a priest?

But perhaps there is liberty here too. Priests may have lost much of the deference associated with those in authority; but with this comes the opportunity to come alongside people as servants and fellow travellers. These troubling times may also bring rain to refresh the roots of what it means to be a priest. If priests are no longer people to look up to, might it become easier for them to hold another's gaze on equal terms? Like the stranger met on the Emmaus Road, priests are better placed to open the word of God spoken through life when they walk the same path as those they accompany. Companions share the bread of common experience; a priest blesses, breaks and shares this precious food to reveal the hidden presence and activity of God.

When the roots become dry, they must go deeper to seek the living water of the Spirit. We depend on the giving of the 'lord of life'. Hopkins' prayer goes to the heart of the life and ministry of a priest: *O thou lord of life, send my roots rain.*

2

Under Pressure

The apostles gathered around Jesus, and told him all that they had done and taught. He said to them, 'Come away to a deserted place all by yourselves and rest a while.' For many were coming and going, and they had no leisure even to eat.[1]

The day after my ordination as a deacon I looked in the mirror. Nothing visible had changed. The dog collar signified the crossing point into a new way of life, but the person wearing it still wore familiar frown lines, and gazed back with the same wary eyes.

There was – I sensed – some interior shift at the level of my confidence. Having said my 'yes' to God, I trusted that God would honour my consent by being there for me in whatever the future held. My uncertainties had found a place to rest in the clear purpose of serving others and opening up within them pathways to God. Without ever voicing it, I carried with me the assumption that my life was now other-centred. My anxieties and needs remained. But long years of preparation, the laying on of hands and anointing with oil cemented my belief that I was now commissioned to be a living expression of the care and presence of God, whose kindness had worked such transformation in my own life. This could be cast as arrogance; who was I – with all my insecurities – to attempt to sort out other people's lives? I didn't see it that way. Serving others was the clear consequence of God choosing me to be a priest and my choice to go with this orientation. Whatever inward troubles and challenges I might face in the future were between me and God, or me and me. I was not complete – and knew this – but God would work through my weakness, and my own needs would somehow be taken care of.

---

[1] Mark 6.30–31.

That was November 1981. My year as a deacon took me – between studies – to an inner-city parish in London. There I was initiated into the strange ways of presbytery living. At breakfast time the parish priest read *The Times*, one assistant *The Telegraph*, another *The Daily Mirror*, while I read the cereal packet. We were very different people thrown together by circumstance under a single roof. Relationships in the house sometimes fizzed with critical spirit beneath a veneer of Christian politeness. In the parish, the ordinary of life was the unexpected. I remember the children I took to a park, who shrank in fear before an open space wider than they had ever experienced before racing round in delirious delight. There was the wonder of watching the gradual healing of a traumatized woman through her reaching out to God. There were the people who came up in the communion queue and asked for money instead of bread. The memories remain vivid. The world was full of God and I was aware of living on the edge – and sometimes beyond where I had previously assumed the edge lay. The real often seemed surreal. Nervousness about the safety of the weekly collection meant everyone had to be involved in taking it by car to the bank on a Monday morning. One priest got out to scan the street for possible danger before the others bundled the money bags into the safe arms of the cashiers. Where were our dark glasses, shoulder holsters and guns? As multicultural as the parish was, on Saturday nights there was always Irish music and dancing in the church hall. I skulked on the edge of the dance floor, doing my duty of talking to everyone while keeping a wary eye out for one particular woman who liked nothing better than to fling me around to steps I didn't know. Perhaps that is a picture for how the whole experience felt: this was a wholly different dance from anything I had ever experienced. I was alive, but dizzy with the unpredictability of it all.

Ordination to the priesthood was followed by some years in a seaside parish in Kent and then a return to inner London. These latter years began to prise open my locked away needs and emotions. I had grown up in a family where feelings were rarely expressed and quickly retreated from. But here what was going on for people inside was often externally obvious: anger, pain, laughter and hurt – all on the street, or at my door, or on the landings and corridors between flats. Poverty was real, violence was visible, and love and friendship loudly celebrated. The intensity began to overwhelm my well-formed defences. The demands made of me summoned up my own human needs. They called out to be noticed; sometimes they spilled out in my relationships with others. I continued to give whatever care and attentiveness I was capable of offering. I spoke of the compassion of God and meant every word I uttered. I accepted that being a priest meant a celibate life, but suffered from my lack of belonging anywhere. I questioned whether God was always to be found in the way the Church I represented expressed itself. I felt angry and frustrated with politicians who denied the reality of the hardship so many experienced and then added a further burden by suggesting they were culpable for their condition. I broke and shared the bread of Eucharist and Word and found within them healing for myself and for those I served. I never imagined leaving the priesthood. And then one day I crossed a hitherto unseen line of what was possible for me.

Reading over that last paragraph you might conclude that being a priest was a misery for me, and in that sense I am better out of it. But it was a rich and necessary time too. I learned so much about lives so different – and yet related – to my own. I travelled deeper into who God is for me and who I am for God. I was involved in work that corresponded with my heart, and in a different way that work continues in my life now. The crisis that widened in me was to do with everything that had formed me as a human being as much as the particular context of being a priest. However, at a remove from the immediate experience I can see that what also made life difficult for me was a series of unexamined expectations I had of myself – or others had of me – directly linked with priesthood.

Beyond my own story, I continue to see the heavy weight of such demands affecting the lives of priests from different traditions. It is these that I will now examine, exploring both their sources and their impacts. Understanding – and when necessary challenging – the distortions these expectations bring will help remove the disabling burdens that sometimes attach themselves to the experience of being a priest. There will always be pressure, and pressure can be life-giving – or proof of being alive. But sustained pressure, built around false assumptions, can begin to wear away at our spirit and narrow our opening to the Holy Spirit.

A priest is always available

Sleep ended when the phone rang. It was 5.30 am. Fumbling in semi-darkness I grasped the receiver and spluttered a weary greeting. 'Hello, Father,' a bright voice spoke, 'I thought I'd ring you now before you got too busy.' I am not sure whether I went on to say 'thank you' for such thoughtfulness.

One of the challenges of being a priest is the way it tends to define the whole of one's existence. Commonly we view priesthood as more than a job. The role is not put down at the end of the working day. And when is the end – or beginning – of the working day? The switch between on time and off time is unreliable. Beyond mere boundaries of time a priest is a priest, and with this comes internal and external expectation of availability. A priest is there to serve others, to listen to their needs, and to be alongside them in times of trouble. The phone rings; the doorbell summons; there is no one else to answer the call.

Where did I pick up this notion of the ever-available priest? The journey began long before the seminary. A priest's life was dedicated to God. He (it was always a 'he') wore different clothes. Of course he would have had a life before ordination, but in a child's eye it was difficult to imagine this. A priest wasn't really a person in the normal understanding of the word; he was 'Father'. 'Father' might be friendly or scary; he might surprise you by coming into the playground and kicking round a football and he might warn you of the ever-present dangers of 'mortal sin'. If he came to the house (and what a commotion that caused!) he was to be shown into the front room where no one ever sat, and given tea in a cup that no other person drank from. A priest was always a priest and therefore always available.

As years passed, priests began to come down from the pedestals erected for them. They became more human and approachable. But they were always priests. My own draw towards priesthood mingled with my attraction to the person of Jesus. Jesus was always there for people. He noticed the one at the back of the crowd. He made time for each person. There was no limit to his giving, even to the cost of his life. This purity of focus in serving others appealed to me; perhaps, without recognizing it, I saw this as a way of integrating my fractured being into a useful whole. At the seminary I cannot recall ever being told that as a priest I had to be constantly available to others; if anything I might have been warned against it – but somewhat half-heartedly. The larger picture remained one of dedicated self-gift. The crucifix loomed large over the chapel. Ordination defined my life as an offering to God of my time, energy and gifts for others. I would strive to be there for people when they needed me.

Knowing myself a little more, I can now see how far my own personal needs interweaved with my determination to be available. I had a great need to justify my existence on planet Earth by proving my usefulness to others. I also lived in fear of possible rejection should I dare to say 'no' to any request made of me. This was an almost lethal combination for anyone going into ministry! Yet these are not uncommon traits among priests. Motivations for saying 'yes' become entangled. God is there for everyone, always – and generously. As a priest of God should I not respond in that same way? The desire to care also flows from our own experiences of weakness, struggle and pain: we want to be there where we know help is most needed. And perhaps we also need the affirmation that our presence makes a difference. So in my case, I responded and responded, and answered politely when the phone rang at 5.30 am. I interrupted my days off to visit those I knew who were struggling just now. And hadn't ordination given me a superpower, meaning I could live in this crazy way and come up smiling?

There were days off, and weeks of holiday. It's good to get away – essential to get away. I remember one day off when I had nowhere clear to go. I was up in my room. No one else was in the house. The doorbell was incessant. Eventually I sat low on the floor so no one could see me. In the *Spiritual Exercises*[2] Ignatius Loyola suggests that when we are moving headlong in ways that are destructive the only way God can grab our attention is through making a loud noise: we get ill; we become worn out and collapse; we grow resentful; we are pulled up by another's observation of the harm we are doing ourselves and beginning to inflict on others. In my case I got angry. A thunderstorm was gathering inwardly, building its oppressive atmosphere. Prayer did not seem to work any more. I would sit in the church and have nothing to say. I smiled and listened in the company of parishioners

---

[2] Exx 335.

but raged against uncooperative machinery and trains that were cancelled. Finally the storm broke and I had it out with God: 'You ask me to look after everyone else but what about me! I have needs too and who is looking after those?' I was all on the side of the older brother of the prodigal:

> 'Listen! For all these years I have been working like a slave for you, and I have never disobeyed your command; yet you have never given me even a young goat so that I might celebrate with my friends.'[3]

With my outburst new light began to break in. I began to see that it wasn't God doing this to me; I was the one responsible. My service had become forced labour. I had exalted my capacity to save others, while showing complete lack of care for my own wellbeing. I fed all who had need and sent myself hungry away. I had become a slave to my own need to be needed, and made God out to be my slave-driver. But now I understood that God wanted me to come in from the fields and join in the party: 'Son, you are always with me, and all that is mine is yours.'[4]

Changing my patterns, and cooperating with God's desire that I begin the work of loving my neighbour by looking after myself, was a slow, faltering process. There was my first 'no', issued in response to an expectation that I put my own needs behind what was convenient for others. I also recognized the importance of using the 'on, off' switch. There had to be limits on my availability: days off that were genuine days off; times of the day when I got out and went elsewhere. Now and then I began to take off my well-worn 'saviour of the world' badge. I caught myself more often in using the language of 'shoulds, oughts and musts' and recognized the need to freely choose whatever I did. But the resistance was strong. The leanings of my own personality and history were deeply grooved into my attitudes and patterns of behaviour. The power of that vision of the saviour-priest, rising above personal needs in total availability towards others, appealed to the idealist in me and had been a consistent element of my formation.

---

[3] Luke 15.29.
[4] Luke 15.31.

The embrace of celibacy was part of that formation. I am not sure that those who make the commitment always see it as an 'embrace', but I, with others, understood there was no way to be a Catholic priest without it, and I worked to make it an active choice that set me free to care for others, rather than an imposition thrust upon me. Explicitly or implicitly, celibacy was linked with availability. A priest would have no other call on their time and attention, with the assumption that this could only be good. The woman who phoned me at 5.30 am 'before I got too busy' understood this link all too clearly! A danger of celibacy, for me at least, was this suggestion that any human being can always be on call without harm to their physical, mental and spiritual welfare. The guidance given to those preparing for, or practising, celibate ministry may have changed since my time, with greater emphasis placed on boundaries and making time for oneself; but actions and attitudes can also flow from what we unconsciously infer. For the outsider making their request, and for priests themselves, celibacy seems to suggest availability – even availability without bounds.

It is not my task or intent here to pass judgement on the discipline of celibacy within the Catholic tradition. I do, however, urge caution on those who link celibacy with availability. What harm might this association result in for those who swallow the message whole? How helpful is it to give the impression to the wider public that priests have no other life other than their ministry? Those who live a celibate life within a religious community have the rhythms of common life to help safeguard against extremes of activity. The heartbeat of the *Rule of Saint Benedict* is balance. The hours of the day allow proper time for work, rest, prayer, meals and study. Celibate priests outside religious communities lack such clear boundaries; there is no bell to tell them to move away from what they are doing, and often no person to keep their lives in check.

What of those priests who have partners, and perhaps children? There are other pulls on their attention. This can help provide a necessary balance to a priest's life that grounds their ministry rather than detracts from it. However, the draw towards availability as a priest may create other hazards. What call on time has priority? The larger danger here is not that a priest lacks availability; it is that she or he neglects those key relationships that underpin their life and work. The dice are in some way loaded. To be a priest is to be there for other people, following the example of Christ. A priest is at the heart of the life of the faith community. A priest has to show interest – at least – in all that is going on. A priest has a calling from a 'higher' authority. It's easy to justify putting ministry first with the hope that family will be able to make do until a time comes when the work is less demanding – except that this quiet time never quite arrives. As a married person still working for the Church, though not as a priest, I often took those closest to me for granted while I followed my 'calling'. Perhaps it is only now that I see that my calling also concerns my availability to my family and friends. For the life of God is about relationship: this is the heartbeat of every vocation. And what better place can there be to learn how to relate with love and attention than with those closest to us? There are times in the Gospels when Jesus turned away from the demands of his family to be present to the crowd who looked to him for teaching and healing. But rather than putting one group above the other, my sense is that Jesus was moved to show that each was deserving of care. In another moment, Jesus puts his entire work at risk by deciding to go to the aid of his friend Lazarus. How much time did Jesus spend loving into being his most intimate companions through time set apart from the needs of the crowd? How much did he himself need those times?

Generosity doesn't have to be exhausting

Celibate, or bonded together with another in a lifelong partnership, how do we begin to find balance, and a healthy and life-giving attitude towards availability? This is a practical question, and it is also a spiritual one. What kind of God do we serve?

Generosity is at the heart of God, but generosity doesn't have to be exhausting. The Trinity is a creative flow of giving *and* receiving, a spring of life that never runs dry because it is continually replenished. All that has being is the creative overflow of this mutual exchange of life. Made in the image of God, we are invited to give of ourselves, but also – and equally generously – open ourselves to receive. This is the God-life priests are called to celebrate with their people and pronounce with their words and actions. It has a distinctive shape that asks to be lived, where all have an equal right of flourishing and all have a duty of care. A one-sided giving fails to express the fullness of the life of God as Trinity. It also conveys a lopsided view of what it means to be Church. Any model based on a fixed relationship between performer and audience, or provider and recipients, misses the point of who God is and what God does. The same Spirit that flows between Father and Son overflows in all created being and animates our relationships. We flourish and create in and through one another. Since all share this one Spirit, all pour out life and all open themselves to be enlivened.

In one inner-city church I worked in I helped start a music group. As there were a number of young people who wanted to join in we bought some guitars and I passed on the few chords I had thus far mastered. After ten weeks most of them were better guitarists than I had become in ten years. An accordion player joined and then came those who could play flutes. At Sunday Mass they accompanied and led the singing. It was beautiful to witness their young lives pouring out and lifting the whole congregation in song. They began to teach me a few more chords. When I practised with them I felt alive in the energy of music made together. In such ways we are granted glimpses of the unending creativity of God's life: each one drawing the other out; making a joyful noise in communion with one another. Generosity doesn't have to be exhausting. You don't have to play all the chords on your own.

Saying 'yes' and saying 'no'

Attitudes towards availability will also be shaped by personality, upbringing and the process of formation. As a priest it is wise to stop now and then and ask oneself, 'Where do I place myself in the pecking order of care?' An answer comes from reflecting on actual actions, attitudes and patterns rather than what we theoretically aspire to. We might be looking out with perception and sensitivity to the needs of other people, while resolutely remaining deaf and blind to what is happening in our own life. If someone inclines towards selfishness then it is helpful for them to push beyond gratifying their own needs through generosity towards others. But for those who habitually neglect themselves in the pursuit of remaining available, the daunting challenge will be to sometimes put themselves first. The attitudes that drive self-neglect may be slow to change; but honouring one's own needs through practical action begins this process of inner balancing. What might this mean? Giving time to be with friends whose company energizes rather than drains you; making space for the recreational activities that wake your spirit: painting, line dancing, motorbike riding, thriller reading, planting seeds, or walking the Pennine Way. Wasting time now and then as you gaze at clouds scudding through the sky, or you listen to the slow heartbeat of the moving sea; allowing God to waste some time with you.

You will also need to cultivate the art of saying 'no'. As one who has struggled to say this very short word, I have a few suggestions:

Before you say 'yes', consider what you are thereby saying 'no' to
For example, if I say 'yes' to this request am I saying 'no' to my own needs at this moment for needful rest or recreation? Every 'yes' implies a 'no' – and conversely every 'no' implies a 'yes' (for example, a 'yes' to expressing in action that your wellbeing matters too).

When possible give yourself space before making a commitment
Jesus himself delayed some time before going to the aid of his friend Lazarus. Time allows room to discern what approach is appropriate, and to consider whether the response we are inclined to is being moved by God or by our own insecurities. Remember that 'no' and 'yes' in themselves are words of neutral and equal value; one response is not more Christian than the other.

Give reasons for refusing a request where necessary but don't be led into making excuses
Keep your responses simple, honest and straightforward. If something doesn't feel right but you say, 'I can't come today because I am busy', the likely response is, 'Well, can you come tomorrow?' You will run out of excuses!

Learn to be hospitable

Another word for availability is hospitality; but not the hospitality that seeks to impress by the superior quality of the table furnishings and the untold courses of the meal. You are not here to provide a 24-hour-a-day restaurant; you are here to be at home – and through being at home to have the room within yourself to welcome guests. This is what God desires for all, priest or lay. We have to do the hard work of allowing God to be generous with us: to make time for prayer, and time for whatever refreshes our spirit. The moment to serve will come, but first we must consent to be served. If hospitality is not to become mean or measured it has also to be received. This might go against the grain of all our expectations and start to unravel our inherited beliefs about what gives us worth. But begin by making yourself at home as the honoured guest of a generous host; there is no other way.

Justification by busyness

Imagine the time and place: a group of priests together in conversation. Perhaps it is coffee before the deanery meeting begins. 'How's it going?' one asks. 'It's OK, but I have got so much on – three funerals in the last week, the building committee tonight and school governors tomorrow,' comes the reply. Now hear another conversation: 'How's it going?' one asks. 'Life is good,' the other says. 'Things are really quiet; I haven't got much to do.'

Aside from whether life as a priest in a parish setting can ever be *that* quiet, how often do you hear priests talking about the spaces in their lives? My experience is that priests tend to suffer from competitive busyness. When in company with their peers – unless they have previously developed a high level of mutual trust – they feel the pressure to justify their worth by showing how full their day is. And often, of course, it is: meetings, services, building problems, people at the door, emails – the list goes on. That level of demand can be an issue in itself. Here, though, I want to explore that pressure priests often experience to justify their worth by demonstrating how busy they are.

In the first place it should be said that seeking justification by busyness is not the sole preserve of priests. We live in a fast, 'happening' world, obsessed with the immediacy of connection with people and the next event on the calendar. The sophistication of mobile devices means we are continually confronted by tasks – be they conversations or work. There was a time when escape from the office meant just that: it was possible to be unavailable. There are fresh ways to assess one's significance: how many 'friends' do I have on social media? How many people have looked at the website since yesterday? The more connections a person has seems to suggest to what degree they are at the pivot points of where life is happening. Busyness becomes equated with personal significance and success. Technologies compete to find ways life can happen faster, with greater capacity to do several things at once.

We are all being schooled in the art of juggling, some more successfully than others. The current popularity of mindfulness –

inside and outside faith communities – suggests more and more people want to find a way to get off the high speed travelator. The cost of living this way is too high. Priests are not immune from the same pressures. It's like arriving at a mainline station at rush hour and attempting to move against the flow of human traffic. You are neither seen nor given room; the human tide is moving on automatic and you are in its way.

Priests may also be in the thrall of justification by busyness through anxiety about their worth. As I have already outlined, we live in a capitalist culture that places high value on productivity and achievement. It's hard to avoid measuring ourselves against others: 'Am I a good product? Do I deliver effective outcomes?' At the very least we want to be able to demonstrate a high level of activity. It is inevitable that when priests gather together they will 'talk shop'. We need a space where we can air what is going on for us with people who share our way of life. But it is good to remember that the world of 'shop', with its talk of customer numbers, productivity and profit, is not the be all and end all of the kingdom of God.

Sometimes busyness is unavoidable: there is a lot to do and at this moment it falls to me to do it. As a way of life busyness is corrosive of human spirit and may close us to Holy Spirit. Priests become driven people rather than disciples who are attentive and responsive to God's leading. The primary way of expressing the reality of God becomes ceaseless activity. Does God demand busyness in his name? It's not a long journey before we reach a point where God becomes the most demanding and inconsiderate of bosses, requiring more productivity from limited human resources. And if the workers should complain, let them make bricks without straw![5]

In a fractured, fast world where many feel driven, their freedom lost, the challenge to priests is to live and model rest – not as an alternative to activity but as its source. Relationship with God is our resting place: a still point from where all movement comes – just as the formless void and darkness became the stage for God's creating, naming and blessing.[6] What priests – and all Christians – are called to, is not frenetic piling up of deeds, but cooperation with the Spirit

---

[5] Exodus 5.6–7.
[6] Genesis 1.2.

that blows where it chooses.[7] Such responsiveness flows from attentive pausing; we wait to see where the wind is moving. We seek to work together with God, rather than ask God to bless the great assembly of our works.

---

[7] John 3.8.

Am I meeting my targets?

We live in a world of targets, strategic development plans and performance reviews. The rise and fall of companies' fortunes is at least in part dependent on the effectiveness of these processes of planning and evaluation. There was a time when Church structures stood aloof from such worldly vanities. With its focus on things eternal and the workings of grace, the Church went on its way without having to worry too much about results. In a capricious world, largely beyond human control, most people invested in one god or another and allied themselves to an associated faith community. But things have changed. Now humanity generally feels more confident in moderating and fixing the ways of the universe in accordance with its needs. We have more of a handle on how to keep ourselves warm and fed. To an extent at least, God has been sidelined; we can manage quite well on our own, thank you. Sunday attendance in most Christian churches in the West has fallen dramatically in the last 50 years. Income is less certain; faith institutions are under very practical pressures.

Slowly – and behind time – Churches have gained the humility to learn from the secular world. It makes practical sense to evaluate needs, to assess available resources and to deploy these as effectively as possible. Practitioners become more effective when they are supported in learning from their experience and revising attitudes and methods as a result. In one sense this is nothing new. Jesus had a clear sense of mission or purpose. He thought strategically in the sense of choosing others to share this work and helping them learn from what they were experiencing. He sent out 70 in pairs with precise instructions and on their return evaluated with them what had taken place.[8]

I have worked in a variety of roles within church-related institutions. At times I was frustrated by the lack of strategic thinking; at other points I felt overwhelmed by the amount of it. Churches either seem to neglect sensible planning methods or swallow them entire and whole, irrespective of whether or not they fit the reality on the ground or the values of the kingdom. In many church contexts, diminishing congregations, declining income, growing demands

---

[8] Luke 10.1–20.

on expenditure, and reduced numbers of those in ministry have led to a stronger emphasis on performance and achievement. Are congregation numbers growing or declining? Is the income from giving meeting targets? Are there any young people in the church on Sunday mornings? What do the answers to these questions say about the performance of the priest?

What happens to the priest who is working hard, being creative in approach, looking to make the most of available resources and is seeing no growth? Is this personal failure, institutional malfunction or cultural change; or are we asking the wrong questions or using the wrong measures? What tends to happen is that the priest as the person on the spot absorbs the pressure. Even when visible decline flows from factors far beyond a priest's power to control, they are likely to feel responsible. The wear and tear of being the one on the ground when the life of a church building or congregation becomes unsustainable is almost immeasurable. The loss, anger and insecurity of church members have to go somewhere, and more often than not those emotions fly at the priest, who must somehow process them and keep going.

Measures of achievement will never – by themselves – sit comfortably with the story at the heart of Christian faith: the mission of the preacher from Nazareth and his journey to renewed life through rejection and a cruel death. Ministry has to reserve a sacred space for what others might see as failure. This is not to say that priests should be passive and fatalistic in the face of difficulty. There is room for creative thinking, strategy and the good use of resources in the service of the kingdom. There are talents to be used, not buried. But there is also no way around the mystery priests celebrate sacramentally through baptism: we plunge into ending, letting go our tight grip of what has been; the waters of death wash over us; we rise to new life.

Jesus' ministry was purposeful and thought through. He urged nothing less on his followers:

> 'See I am sending you out like sheep into the midst of wolves, so be wise as serpents and innocent as doves.'[9]

The serpent assesses the situation and uses imagination to discern

---

[9] Matthew 10.16.

what approach to take. The dove will never be able to defend itself entirely from harm. The challenge for the wider Church is not to inadvertently join the wolves through an undue attachment to success defined along narrowly determined lines. The sheep need practical and immediate support – not least when the situation they are sent into is difficult.

Saviour of the world

It is ridiculous, isn't it, even beginning to think that I might be the saviour of the world. But even without naming or owning the thought it is possible to live out the illusion. It could be the result of overblown ego. But it could also flow from the received pressure of expectation that somehow I should be able to resolve whatever problematic issue or awkward question comes my way: 'I am a priest. I should know what to do or how to fix this.' I remember how useless I felt when someone close to me fell seriously ill: 'I am a person of faith; I preach the goodness of God. I should be able to bring healing to this person. Why can't I do anything? Why aren't you listening to me, God?'

There is a further layer that may also come into play: we expect God to fix things. After all, even if we have to own we have no power to save, God does. So we should expect what is unresolved, messy and difficult to be sorted out in ways we can easily recognize. But then it's not. There is pain that a person carries where we can find no power to heal. There are wrongs done that have lasting impacts – and nothing, it seems, can make them right. There are questions that remain just that: questions … raw, troubling and without answer. We stay alongside another who wonders where God is in this, and why doesn't God do something; we mumble a response as we must, or keep an awkward silence, as the same questions echo in our own minds.

A priest is faced with awful moments when God does not appear to save: conducting a child's funeral; being alongside a family as the life support system of a loved one is turned off. Prayer – however fervent – doesn't always bring the desired result, and the defence that God *has* answered the prayer, but in a way we do not as yet understand, rings hollow. Priests may be caught between two conflicting movements. On the one hand they are pulled by the need to defend God and keep alive the faith of those before them; on the other, they themselves may be hurting and troubled. When everyone else has gone away, they need someone to make it all right for them.

A mechanic fixes cars. A dentist attends to troublesome teeth. Why isn't a priest able to solve spiritual pain? In part, the difference is that priests themselves are not the primary healers; instead they help open the door for those who seek healing to the whole-making love of God. They are John the Baptists, working to lay low the hills and fill in the valleys so that those they minister to can find their way to God. Through their hospitality, attentive listening and leading of prayer they help make tangible the presence of a compassionate God, who cares about people's pain. But they themselves are neither God nor Saviour. A priest is not a dispenser of easy answers. Like anyone else, they must live with what is unresolved.

A mechanic fixes cars. A dentist attends to troublesome teeth. But God does not intervene to solve or prevent our struggles and pains in the immediate moment. Instead God is alongside and within us as we work through our difficulties and live with our losses. The cross is the most inconvenient of symbols for those who seek immediate resolution of suffering. The cross speaks of more than solidarity; it expresses God's active and costly choice to go on bringing resurrection within all dimensions and experiences of life; but the way often lies through some form of death. For a priest, delivery from expectations they might hold that they should have the power to save is often painful; but it is a release. We let go into mystery, and though it continues to trouble us to do so, we come to realize we are letting go into active and resourceful Love.

Immovable faith

One thing a politician cannot do is express doubts about their own stated policies. Faced with a press baying for blood, or an opposition waiting for the smallest of inconsistencies to pounce, they must uphold the party line. The policy is well thought through, the very best of options and destined to bring untold benefits. There is no room – publicly at least – for uncertainty.

What of priests, representing the authority and wisdom of the Church, leading the people in public prayer and the recitation of the Creed? Can they waver? The parallels are not exact – and I hope to demonstrate why they are different – but the pressures felt may be similar. What happens if, as a priest, I am no longer sure about the gospel I preach, or the God I once believed in, or the spiritual path I once advocated and sought to live? A priest has private thoughts and public responsibilities. Sometimes the two clash. What do I do if I have a responsibility to lead people in prayer and to encourage them in deepening their relationship with God, if I no longer know how to pray? How do I bring God's comfort to others if I experience no such comfort myself?

At the heart of such anxieties is a particular understanding of what constitutes faith. Is faith absolute certainty about revealed truths and how they have been previously stated or understood? Are faith and doubt opposites, or are they necessary companions? For a politician, stated faith in the party's policy is an unwavering assertion of the effectiveness of what is proposed and the accuracy of the assessment on which it rests. There can be no room for doubt. A politician understands (or purports to understand) what is going on and what action is needed. They must speak with authority even when met with widespread scepticism. Inwardly they may well have doubts about what is proposed, but there is no room for external expression of these. They must not crack. They must be assertive of the truth of their claims and defend their stated beliefs with all the power they can muster. How is this similar to, or different from, the stance taken by a priest?

Faith in a Christian sense centres on trust rather than certainty, and relationship more than policy. Faith is a willing choice to trust

God in the midst of uncertainty. Abraham, the father of faith, sets out for a land he does not know in response to God's invitation. The disciples respond to Jesus' invitation to follow him, even though nothing is said about where the road will lead or what will take place along the way. At the heart of the work of priests is the responsibility to develop and nurture the faith of those they minister to. What does this mean? A priest may feel under pressure to shore up all doubts and instruct those they guide in sure and certain truths. But in doing so are they nurturing faith, or fearful clinging to certainty? The work of developing faith involves sharing those beliefs that flow from the experience of those who have walked these paths before. There is a place for creeds. We need landmarks. But nurturing faith also involves encouraging a spirit of daring and adventure in response to God's invitation to relationship. Priests can help with map reading: through their theological and scriptural education they have the tools to help make sense of where a person stands and what direction the road might lead from here. But sustaining another's faith also involves the willingness to stay alongside people as they move deeper into the mystery of who God is, who they are, and what this means for their lives. Priests also travel along this road of vulnerable trust, where revelation is a continuing process rather than a finished work.

Recently a retired priest shared his experience of reviewing his time in parish ministry as he went on a walking pilgrimage. The first image of the Church that came to mind was that of the Sealed Knot Society: a group of people who regularly dress up and re-enact events within the Civil War of the mid-seventeenth century. Was that what he had been facilitating? Then came the image of a boat moored securely to the quay. Safe from wind and wave, it rested secure, without venturing out onto the dangerous waves it was intended for. Perhaps most tellingly, the physical and emotional experience of the pilgrimage itself began to be in dialogue with his experience of priesthood. A pilgrim sets out intentionally seeking a destination. That much is known. What cannot be wholly predicted or controlled is the experience of the walk itself: the people met, the physical impact on the body of walking, the challenges of the terrain, the clarity or otherwise of the path. A pilgrim chooses, each day, to be open – and vulnerable – to these uncertainties. Whatever plan he or she has made will at some stage be unpicked by circumstances beyond anticipation. This – for the walking priest – felt a more authentic expression of faith: the chosen orientation of one's being towards God and the resulting disorientation. The journey is marked by unanticipated gift, joy and surprise, and also confusion, pain and uncertainty.

A priest is not one who belongs in the spiritual arrivals lounge: the journey completed and all uncertainties resolved. A priest is a spiritual traveller, as are all who choose to seek meaning in relation to what is larger than themselves. Meeting these challenges with honesty and humility provides the words and actions of a priest with authenticity. A priest, in struggling yet choosing to go on, has something to say to those who also have doubts, questions and uncertainties. A politician needs a ready and definite answer. A priest will sometimes admit 'I do not know; I do not understand; I have no answer'. Priests live close to mystery: the dying and rising of their Lord, the transcendence and immanence of their God, the endings and beginnings of earthly life.

There is a further layer of challenge likely to emerge at some point in one's ministry: what if a conflict arises between the way a priest has come to understand how God is in relationship with humankind and the stated practices or policies of the Church? To what degree can I publicly represent the Church – as my position as a priest asks of me – if I have come to believe in my own heart that in this matter the Church is wrong? For as long as I was able I might seek to wriggle around the conflict, avoiding the area as best I could or diverting the conversation away from situations where I might be asked to defend the practice. But what happens on the day when I am put on the spot and I cannot turn away? I remember running the RCIA (Rite of Christian Initiation of Adults) process in the last parish I served. One year everyone who came forward seeking baptism or to be received into communion with the Catholic Church was either divorced and remarried, or living together outside marriage. Under Church discipline none of them were in a position to receive the Eucharist. And yet they were all people seeking God, with lively and developing faith. There was possible recourse through marriage, or by seeking the annulment of previous unions and the 'regularization' of the current relationship. But I was still left with the question: 'Why do we do this?' If Jesus sat down and ate with those others labelled tax collectors and sinners, why do we turn people away? I felt torn between different dimensions of priestly ministry. I recognized that as a priest I represented the Church's teaching authority, but as a pastor and nurturer of faith, I could not defend the Church's discipline in this matter. At the most fundamental level it went against my own experience and understanding of the nature of God.

I share this not to argue a case, but to illustrate the tensions priests may experience between their representative role and their personal beliefs. In a previous generation within the Catholic Church, priests working within contexts of severe poverty and injustice found themselves caught between their draw towards a theology of liberation and loyalty to a Church nervous of where such a movement might lead. Within the Anglican Church in recent years, debates around attitudes towards people in same sex relationships have caused significant anguish. For some priests the questions concerned have personal significance: how does the Church view my relationship? Compromises between publicly stated positions and private practice often rest uneasily.

Where is the balance to be reached between respect for the representative function a priest holds in relation to the teaching authority of the Church and personal conscience? Can there be a balance, or does each priest have to find their own way of living the contradictions? It seems to me that a priest is often at the sharp end of the struggles of a Church that is both institution and a pilgrim people. Clear regulation and guidance are necessary, but so is openness to the Spirit in the face of emerging challenges and untrodden ground. A priest at a local level represents both sides of the struggle. Pastoral encounters ask questions not addressed in theological handbooks. Perhaps a beginning in easing the pressure is to accept that sometimes this is how it will be. Nothing has gone 'wrong'. Such struggles are the stuff of faith. Priesthood is shaped in such a way that personal conflicts of these sort are likely to arise.

Larger questions remain as to how priests are supported in working through – or living with – the contradictions inherent within their role. A good spiritual director can provide one safe space to air the tension and explore where the Spirit leads. Given that these conflicts revolve around the tension between the expressed position of the Church and pastoral practice, priests also need safe spaces where their struggles can be aired, heard and taken seriously by those in authority within the Church. What has sometimes happened in the past is that an individual priest has been ignored, condemned or written off through a perceived failure to work through the contradictions and come up with the approved answer. The pilgrim journey is not easy for anyone, and certainly not so for the institutional Church. We have to face the challenges together, rather than disowning them for their inconvenience. Another parallel may help. A scientist does research and comes up with evidence that conflicts with the current consensus of understanding within the scientific community. Naturally there is a current of resistance to the findings; reputations and the truth of previous studies are at stake. A typical response might be to suggest that there are flaws in the research methods used; and indeed there might be. However, science progresses through evidence that refuses to fit current theories. Taking the findings seriously may set new questions. In turn, these questions give birth to new enquiry, and the eventual deepening of understanding. The people at the experimental forefront of research must be listened to, or science begins to die. At every level the Church has to find a deeper level of security that rests not in avoiding uncertainty, but embracing it; for it is here that trust grows. The questions that priest-adventurers carry within themselves must be welcomed and heard. They should not bear their struggles alone.

Living with difficult people

Priests often wear a dog collar around their necks; they rarely wear haloes around their heads. There are so many difficult people and sometimes they gather together in clumps: 'My curate is impossible.' 'The church warden makes my life a misery.' 'When I am with that group I want to scream!'

It is hard for a priest to scream; it's not the done thing. Priests are expected to be understanding, even-tempered and unerringly welcoming. No wonder people are disappointed. Who did I find most difficult? On some days it was the sheer pressure of people wanting and needing attention *now*. My energy became sapped; I wasn't always as open and tolerant as I aspired to be. At one time I had a series of anonymous phone calls. I answered only to be met by silence. Ten minutes would pass and then the phone would ring again ... more silence. The pattern continued. At last I lost my cool and shouted down the phone, 'For heaven's sake, tell me what you want or stop ringing.' A pause followed and then the cultured voice of my bishop informed me that he was phoning to pass on details of his parish visitation. There was a received tradition of answering the phone by giving the name of the church: 'St Joseph's' perhaps, or 'All Saints'. My church was 'Our Lady of the Immaculate Conception'. It dawned on me at some point that I might be giving the wrong impression about who was on the other end of the line! In any case there was little that was immaculate or saintly about my responses on a fraught day. By and large I worked hard at being accommodating and friendly in my contacts with people. As a priest I wanted to show a welcoming face and to give each person proper attention. I hoped to be an open door to the hospitable and gentle God I believed in through the way I received people. Some people, however, had the uncanny knack of bringing out my worst: a woman whose display of piety ran at odds with her treatment of other people; a man who talked and talked and talked and was a self-proclaimed authority on all things. Even if my irritation or frustration was largely contained, it was still there. A brisk walk or a run provided some means to pound out feelings on a pavement.

I suspect many priests feel the pressure of maintaining a

response that is kind and tolerant. It goes with the territory of seeking to reflect something of God's positive regard for each person, and as such it is an appropriate behavioural orientation. But it won't always work. It is natural to warm to some people more than others. Some people remind us of difficult people in our own past and so carry for us a double load of uncomfortable feelings. Sometimes people are unreasonable, mean or downright destructive. Sometimes we have had enough.

I have listened to more than one priest who has effectively been bullied by a key figure in their congregation. I have certainly heard the struggles of priests with their own close colleagues. It is unreasonable to expect of oneself an unlimited capacity to grin and bear it. Everyone needs release now and then, and if it's not appropriate or helpful to share what is felt within the immediate context, there have to be some safe spaces where this can be done.

Priests also need to remove their own imaginary haloes. Perfection of behaviour will always be out of reach. Ordination proves not to be an inoculation against irritation. The orientation towards tolerance, hospitality, understanding and generosity is important. The universal practice of the same is impossible. Illusions of self-made loveliness crumble and die; we see we are a naked human being after all. Ministry as a priest seems set up to show us that not only are there difficult people out there, but we too are of their number.

If we allow our reflection to lead us beyond the monstrous faults of others, we begin to see in our reactions and responses our own jagged edges and vulnerable places. The temptation then might be to turn against ourselves, pronouncing guilt and sentence for our own weakness. But the more useful truth is that we too are people in need of compassion, forgiveness and grace. We need to be believed in and loved in our rawness. We need God.

Some years ago Henri Nouwen drew on the image of the risen Christ to describe how those who minister in his name are wounded healers.[10] There is nothing romantic about the term. Wounds hurt. But wounds begin to heal when we take our gaze away from ourselves

---

[10] Henri J. M. Nouwen, 1979, *The Wounded Healer: Ministry in Contemporary Society*, London: Penguin Random House.

and meet God's gaze of love in the eye. I have used the language of nakedness and rawness and this is how it seems. We remove the clothes of our imagined perfection; we strip away the mask of self-sufficiency we project to the world. Sometimes these things happen to us without our choosing. We have nowhere to hide; but, in God, we have no further need to hide. This is it. This is me. This is the 'me' you love and go on believing in. Humility of this sort sets free a river of compassion that begins in God, flows to us, and then moves from us to those difficult people.

The struggles remain. We do not stop being difficult and neither do those other awkward people in our lives. Rather than preventing our progress towards wholeness, these encounters open up the possibility of movement towards it through greater self-knowledge and a more willing dependence on the grace of God. God always has room for difficult people.

Omnicompetence

What does a priest do? The ordinal will suggest some answers. Experience will bring others. A priest chairs meetings, worries about finances, puts out a bucket under a leaking roof, meets a grieving family, composes a reflection for the weekly newsletter, picks out the winning tickets in the raffle, presides at the daily Eucharist, frets about the failing heating system and entertains the children at the local school – and that's just Tuesday!

Ordination training can never prepare for such a many-limbed ministry. A priest can even feel ill equipped for what might seem basic tasks. I remember the first baptism I conducted. I felt well versed in the theology but more than hazy about the service itself. Each turn of the page revealed another thing I had to do – all the while attempting to put the family at their ease and not drown the baby. Moved by necessity in contexts where there are fewer priests around, and by theologies grounded in the discipleship of all believers and every-member ministry, expressions of priesthood are changing. The ideal priest is increasingly seen as one who enables the distinctive service of each person, while holding together and coordinating the whole. The skill set required, however, is still a large one. The role requires that priests should be managers and pastors, listeners and teachers, ideas people who also pay attention to details. They should be able to lead worship with sensitivity to time and place, build up links with local groups and agencies and teach people to pray. They are to come alongside the sick of mind and body, and not talk down to children and young people. All this, and when everyone else has gone home, put away the chairs, turn off the lights and answer the late-night phone call.

Where does the priest exist who is naturally good at all of this? And yet a priest can still feel the pressure to show an equal level of competence in every task they encounter, as if ordination conveyed some form of superpower. What can happen – and naturally so – is that priests steer towards those areas where they feel at home and away from tasks where they meet their sense of inadequacy. There are priests who keep themselves in the place of manager, but do little managing, and others who hold on to their role as pastor in chief, but avoid situations where they might have to meet another's vulnerability. My focus here is not the detail of methods of professional development – as valuable as these can be. Instead I want to look at the priest and person who stands before God and comes before people. Here – in the presence of God – there is no other way to be than who we are. Before God, in humility, we can own where our natural gifts lie, give thanks for them and offer them generously. We can also admit our sense of inadequacy; we can meet the fear that steers us away from where we feel uncomfortable. Rather than see our lack as a measure of our worth, we can – with God – look away from ourselves to where true need lies and begin to explore how those needs might be met beyond what we can offer, letting go of any pride or illusion that tells us that we have to be the one and sole resource. We can ask for help from God and from other people. Where there is no other recourse but to be the person who must meet those needs, then we own our fears, ask God's help, do the best we are able, and refrain from beating ourselves up because we cannot offer more.

Taking practical steps to develop skills and confidence in areas where we do not yet have the necessary tools and confidence is one way we cooperate with God's belief in us and God's continued work within us. Ministerial development reviews, training courses and mentoring can all become ways we work with the Spirit in our own growth. Just as important is the humility of making an honest and non-judgemental assessment of our abilities. Asking for help, letting go any expectation of omnicompetence, and working alongside others who possess the experience, qualities and skills we lack are also ways priesthood is exercised well. When we do so we express a God who is Trinity, communion and relationship. Competence rests in the Body of Christ rather than in a single person. We are all in a process of becoming, not just as individuals, but through the weaving of the Spirit. Sought and trusted, God will do more through us than we can ask or imagine.

3

Perspectives on Priesthood

To live in the midst of the world with no desire for its pleasures; to be a member of every family, yet belonging to none; to share all suffering; to penetrate all secrets, to heal all wounds; to daily go from men to God to offer him their homage and petitions; to return from God to men to bring them his pardon and hope; to have a heart of fire for charity and a heart of bronze for chastity; to bless and be blest forever. O God, what a life, and it is yours, O priest of Jesus Christ![1]

My predecessor in the first parish I served as a priest had these words of Lacordaire written large on a poster in his room. The line that drew my attention was 'O God, what a life!'

What is a priest? What is distinctive about priesthood? What happens to a person when they are ordained? In answering these questions assumptions are made; and not all flow from a clear theological grounding. For those who relate in some way to the priest in their parish, perspectives on priesthood will be shaped by present and past experience. What have priests been like? How have they behaved? What has been the quality of their relationship with lay people?

As a child, priests were men (always), Irish (always), in a dog collar (always), sure of themselves (generally), impatient (often). It was hard to imagine that they had ever been anything other than priests. They didn't have names in the way other people in my life did; they were 'Father' first and what followed was almost incidental. I assumed they were completely dedicated to God and had no life other than church services, prayers and parish visiting – outside an

[1] Jean-Baptiste Henri Lacordaire, 1802–61.

occasional trip to the Races. In my early teens, when the thought of becoming a priest first stirred, I struggled to cross the divide between who I was and these firmly set impressions about the character and qualities of priests. Priests were other and different; how could I join their number?

For priests themselves, self-understanding also flows from the nature of the formation they have experienced. As part of my current work I teach a spirituality module for Anglican ordinands in a non-residential theological college. Study sits alongside engagement with the communities and workplaces of which they are a part. How different this is from my own formation, largely enclosed in a seminary set in the Surrey countryside. The separateness of a priest was breathed in, rather than explicitly taught. Apart from a brief day off, holidays and placements, the grounds of the seminary encompassed our whole existence. There was minimal contact with women. The relationships that dominated our lives were with priests and those training to be priests. The eventual donning of clerical dress served to confirm the message implicitly underlined: you are different; you are set apart for God. And yet the length of training and the relative lack of pressure on producing assignments allowed valuable and formative space. For those I now teach, space seems a rare commodity. Does the busyness of their formation unintentionally suggest priesthood is about a full diary and achievement?

The interplay between parishioners and priests may also play a part in a priest's self-understanding. Received expectations begin to form dance steps. If people assume I am always available I might begin to believe that this is the way I should be. If those coming to me expect answers I may find myself slipping into supplying them.

These formative influences are natural and not destructive in themselves. However, if unexamined, they may begin to drive the reactions and responses of priests in ways that build the pressures I have previously described. Particular perspectives on the nature of priesthood will shape how individuals approach sustaining themselves spiritually and emotionally. In what follows I will challenge some commonly held assumptions about what it is to be a priest. You may not find yourself agreeing with everything I suggest, but I hope these thoughts may stimulate your own exploration. If you don't find answers here that satisfy you, I encourage you to go on living with the questions.

A priest is another order of human being through their ordination

Here is my childhood assumption. Priests not only dress differently, they are different. As I grew older, and especially as I began my own preparation for priesthood, the assumption began to dissolve. But did it entirely? At the level of my theoretical understanding, yes: I believed a priest was every bit a human being, as fallible as they come. I disliked anything that smacked of clericalism. I had a running, silent conflict with my first parish priest over the moveable altar rails. I moved them aside; he put them back. I instinctively pulled against the separation of priest and people. My spirit rebelled when I went to celebratory meals where clergy were directed to eat in one space and lay people in another. Before Mass began I sat in the church with the congregation to place myself with God; I was a priest, but like anyone else I understood and experienced that I had to make my way through life and towards God through ordinary human difficulties.

But on the other hand, my attitudes and behaviour demonstrated that I did believe ordination had turned me into a different order of human being. Through my formation and the power of the Spirit's anointing I understood that the sole orientation of my life was to be in service of other people; if it wasn't always so in practice, then it ought to be. There was no space marked out for my own needs. I should – as a priest – have answers about where God was in the messy confusion of life in ways beyond those that might be expected of lay people. I might finger the collar around my neck and prise it loose whenever I could but I was not free to let go of the unlimited availability that I felt a priest ought to offer. I was all too conscious of my weakness, but acted sometimes as if I had some superpower granted only to me as a priest.

As meaningful as ordination is, there is no escape from common humanity. We are in it together. There are no exemptions. Priesthood is a distinctive ministry, vital to the spiritual wellbeing of the people of God. Priests are leaders and servants who gather God's people together around word and sacrament. Priests are also common people with ordinary human needs. There is no other order of person.

Priests have a distinctive spirituality

Is the spirituality of priests distinct from that of lay people? It might depend on what we mean. One way of considering spirituality – from a Christian perspective at least – is a lived response to the work of God in our lives. This lived response can have a particular character related to the nature of the life of those who lead it, or the inspiration of a founding figure or movement. Benedictine spirituality shares much in common with Franciscan spirituality but is also different from it. Benedictines make a promise of stability that holds them in lifelong relationship with a particular group of people under the authority of the abbot or abbess. Franciscans on the other hand are evangelists, following the example of Francis of Assisi who travelled far as a herald of the gospel. For priests outside religious communities there is no one founding figure or detailed rule of life that holds them to a particular expression of lived faith. Arguably this is both strength and weakness. Strength: because priests working in different contexts, drawing from different traditions, and respecting the variety of their personalities, reflect the catholicity of the Church. Priests outside religious communities have freedom to find a pattern of spiritual practice that works for them. Weakness: because without the framework of a meaningful rule of life and a community to hold them to it, priests may flounder. Spiritual practice slips through the net through isolation and the pressure of work. Some find a way and some do not.

There is, however, common ground in terms of the shape of priestly ministry and what stands at its heart: the duty of pastoral care, the task of gathering people together around word and sacrament and equipping God's people for their work of service in the world. There are also common expressions of spiritual practice attached to the life of a priest: a commitment to regular personal prayer, study of the Bible and maintenance of the daily rhythm of the Office. The ministry has a distinct character and purpose that both invites and forms how priests express their lived response to the work of God in their lives. In this sense there is priest-shaped spirituality. Much of the remainder of this book will be devoted to exploring what this spiritual path looks like and the variety of ways it might be expressed. Such a shared understanding of what it means to be a priest and a disciple and how this flows into spiritual practice is vital for the wellbeing of those who undertake this way of life.

Depending on how it is understood, however, there are perils in distinguishing priestly spirituality from that of other people. Historically – in the Catholic Church at least – difference was also often equated with hierarchy. The spiritual path appropriate to lay people was of a very different order to that of the ordained. For lay people, the recitation of formal prayers, participation in the sacraments and the practice of good works was enough. For the ordained, a higher path of devotion beckoned. Given the small number of priests and religious as a proportion of the population it is striking how many of those judged to be saints are of their number. Thankfully, times have changed. Priests often choose to go to lay spiritual directors; retreats are valued by people in all walks of life; at diocesan and local level considerable work is put in to nurture spiritual life within congregations through exploration of different ways of prayer and opening up the riches of different spiritual traditions.

The spiritual paths taken by priests are likely to have common characteristics, since they flow from a way of life that is distinctive. At a more fundamental level ordained and lay share one path. We are all disciples, drawn into a relationship with God that is transformative. This might be seen negatively: what then is distinctive about being a priest? Or it could be viewed positively: *because* it is the same, priests can speak out of their experience and from their heart and find that what they have to say resonates with the lives of those who listen. Because we all follow one who is way, truth and life, priests can also receive encouragement, support and guidance in their discipleship from those who are not ordained.

Priesthood sums up the 'whole' of personal identity

Priests are not alone in having a distinctive uniform. Nurses, police officers, supermarket workers and soldiers are among those who share the habit. For the most part uniforms have no practical function in themselves; true, a soldier's dress might help them blend in with surroundings when on active service, but a priest's attire provides no such camouflage. Uniforms can be useful in symbolic ways: they tell us who's in charge, who to ask or what level of experience or authority an individual holds. The wearing of a uniform reminds the bearer of their role, with its associated responsibilities and codes of conduct.

For most people who wear uniforms there is a moment of relief when it is put aside. A change of clothes marks the end of the working day. The persona demanded of the role can be let go. The person can begin to be 'at home' and be themselves. This is not to say that the uniform tells a lie about who the person is who wears it. Often there is a strong correspondence between what the uniform expresses and the personal values and motivations of the wearer. A police officer might have a strong sense of the importance of justice, law and order. A nurse may have a natural inclination towards caring for others. The uniform, however, does not sum up the totality of the person. It cannot contain or express the complex web of desires, gifts, passions and needs that make up an individual. Nor can a uniform hold within it the whole of a person's history, personality, relationships or circumstances. A uniform is a marker designed for the primary purposes of the organization it represents, rather than a means of self-expression for the individual who wears it. Taking off one's uniform – for an evening, a day off or a holiday – helps us re-engage with the larger picture of who we are.

My sense is that priests find it harder to remove their uniform – and all it carries with it – than other groups. In part this is to do with the lack of definition of the working day. But it also has to do with the tendency to assume that priesthood, and the way of life that flows from it, 'fits' the whole human person of one who is a priest. Priests are not alone in having a strong sense of vocation. However, this sense of personal call carries with it the extra dimension of being drawn by God to this service. Inscribed on the wall of the seminary chapel where I trained were words from the Gospel of John: 'You did not choose me, but I chose you.'[2] That is how it felt for me. I had not chosen a way of life; the way of life chose me; it welled up inside me from God. Whatever conflicts and difficulties arose for me in being a priest, my sense of inward accord with this vocation remained.

This strong sense that being a priest sums up the 'I' – the whole of one's being – is shared by many. But does it? Can it? Priesthood is also a way of life shaped by, and for, the Church. Vocation to the priesthood is – by and large – tested rigorously. Many who feel themselves called to be priests find the road blocked. Those involved in discernment of vocation do test that inner sense of call, but they also have in mind the roles and responsibilities of a priest and the personal qualities this way of life requires. Ultimately decisions are taken not on the basis of whether this role give means for the self-expression of the person, but on whether this person has the capacity to meet the needs of the Church. Alongside these considerations, the Church also determines what categories of people can be priests. In the Catholic Church, a woman with a strong sense of personal call towards priesthood still has nowhere to go.

When – after long struggling – I left the priesthood, I did so with an undiminished sense of vocation to express my being in service of God. Our relationship with God, and our involvement within the world, do not rest entire in any role we hold – even in being a priest. Before and beyond any service we offer, we are called by name as individuals. 'You did not choose me, but I chose you', remains true.

Lest you misunderstand me, being a priest is more than wearing clerical dress. Outward clothing is useful, but counts for little in the end. I am privileged to know priests who have inhabited their role in such a way that the depths of their inner being are expressed in what they do and who they are. The inside and outside correspond. For all this, it is possible for the 'person' to become lost in the 'priest'. For some – at least – the responsibilities of priesthood can become a way of avoiding getting in touch with who they are, perhaps because they fear that this true self is less acceptable than the public face they have grown used to projecting. It is not that a lie is being lived; motivation may remain strong. But it is less than truth. Jesus urges us

---

[2] John 15.16.

not to be afraid of truth – the truth we learn when we make his word about us our home.[3] Seeking this truth is the way of discipleship – a way that sets us free to be all we are for the glory of God. Priests are better priests for allowing God to meet them in their stripped-down humanity.

As much as what we do is important, God also cares about *us*. God bids us rest and play, and express and explore the originality of our creation. This cannot always be done within any function or role, as close as these might be to where our heart lies. Physically or metaphorically, it is important to take the uniform off now and then. It matters to let God deal with us directly as individuals without the clothing of responsibilities and roles. Damage can be done if any group start to see themselves as another species, separate from the ordinary demands and joys of humanity. Humility leads us back to earth, and to the simplicity of being who we are before God and humankind.

A priest has 'arrived' in terms of spiritual development and understanding of personal vocation

Ordination is both ending and beginning. What a journey it is even to get to ordination! There is the first hesitant step of daring to own the glimmer of a draw towards priesthood. Then follow the twists and turns of vocational discernment, and the testing torment of selection interviews. All this merely opens the door to the start of a training and formation process. It can seem a longer and more challenging road than the one that leads to Tipperary. No wonder that, when ordination day comes, there may be a sense of arrival: at last!

Suddenly, after ordination, I am no longer 'Chris', I am 'Father'. People on the receiving end want, or need to believe, that I am a finished product, duly stamped as complete and ready for use. Am I? Along with an eagerness to express new-found knowledge, skills and understanding in meeting the spiritual needs of others, sooner or later a newly ordained priest will discover how much more they still have to learn and grow. We remain disciples: people of the Way. There is further to travel: the call to follow – once heard and responded to

---

[3] John 8.31–32.

– sounds again. We have not arrived; we have begun. We do not yet know who we are or who God is. We have not managed to rest our lives completely in God. Our trust in God has its limits. Salvation has not yet reached down to all in us that is broken, fearful or diminished. We are not able to wholly put aside our self-centredness. We are turning the first pages of our story rather than reading its final lines. Much as another might assume we are sitting in the spiritual arrivals lounge, if we are honest with ourselves we know we are – and always will be – spiritual travellers, urged on as much by our incompleteness as the inward draw of the Spirit.

The same can also be said of our sense of vocation. Are questions about personal calling settled once and for all upon ordination, or do they continue? We might want to put a full stop at the end of the sentence: 'my vocation is to be a priest'. Is it possible to do so? Much will depend on how we understand 'vocation'. Is the end of vocational journeying reached on arrival at a settled state of life, or do questions of calling persist? Peter left his nets and set out on the road with Jesus. This was now the path of his life. His understanding of what it meant to respond to the call of Jesus was turned upside down in the years he walked in his company. The 'follow me' Peter heard by the lakeside after Jesus' death and resurrection had so many more layers of meaning than the one he responded to at the start of his journey. The overall choice remained, but the direction it led him in now was understood very differently; he was to work from his weakness rather than rely on his strength:

> 'Simon, Simon, listen! Satan has demanded to sift all of you like wheat, but I have prayed for you that your own faith may not fail; and you, when once you have turned back, strengthen your brothers.'[4]

Perhaps here is a good point to reflect on your own vocational journey. If you are a priest, what led you towards ordination? Then go a step further: how has your understanding of your vocation as a priest continued to evolve and deepen since ordination? What unexpected paths of ministry have you been led down?

I was around eleven years old when the call began to wake in

4 Luke 22.31–32.

me. I was a regular altar server, inclined to clumsiness but committed to the task. The Catholic church on the edge of town was small and intimate. Entering the back door to the sacristy, a picture of the Sacred Heart of Jesus looked me in the eye. The mingled scents of polish, candle flame and musty books greeted my entry into the church. I lit the candles, checked everything was in its right place. Mass began. The parish priest was a passionate but intimidating figure, with a quick turn of anger and a well of impatience that saw off numerous curates; but he certainly believed in what he was about. The assistant priests who came and went were softer in tone and more approachable. Mass continued; host and chalice were raised and I gazed upwards as I rang the bell, before standing alongside the priest as he distributed communion. It all drew me: the sense of something other and mysterious that I was close to; the priest, set apart from others and intimate with God; the atmosphere of candle flame and incense. But I knew it was impossible for me: after all, to be a Catholic priest you had to be Irish.

That didn't stop other people putting the thought in my head. The nuns were the worst; one had a habit of bending over me with twinkling eye and telling me: 'You would make a wonderful priest.' But I wasn't to be twinkled into the idea – not yet. At 13 I began reading at Mass. Something happened when I stood there: the Word of God came out of me with a sense of confidence and authority that was far from my natural stance in life. I wasn't just reading, I was proclaiming words of life, and felt it. The Bible itself was working this in me. When I received a school prize of any book I wanted I chose the New Testament. Bibles were rarely given place at that time in a Catholic household. Reading about Jesus, I felt a deep attraction. I imagined myself there when he was telling his parables or healing the sick. I was ready for him to see me amid the crowd and call me.

The thought of being a priest was there. I hid it deep, out of view, as best as I could. My fear was that if I mentioned just one word about 'having a vocation' I would be instantly signed up and a collar measured for my neck. There could be no turning back. So I said nothing. In the years that followed I tossed and turned between different possibilities: I would be a priest … I would be a teacher. I fell in love, more than once. University followed. A degree in history might eventually draw me down the path of becoming a teacher. I didn't cope well in the new environment. Socially I felt out of my depth. Academically I couldn't get to grips with what was expected of me. I became agoraphobic. Panic attacks set in when in the company of other people; alone in my room I felt fearful and isolated. Little fingertips of mercy reached out to me; an evangelical Christian who knocked on my door and wasn't put off by my 'I'm a Catholic' defence. He was a gentle soul who combined encouraging me to learn Bible verses by heart with the willingness to sit with me in the gloom of my room. Then there were students from the Catholic Society who invited themselves in for a cup of tea. I knew that whatever they had from their faith that gave them warmth and vitality was what I needed. I reached out to God – more with longing than with words. Over time the awareness grew that I wasn't alone in the battleship grey of my room. Jesus was there – at home in the mess. In the depths of winter, a sensation of warmth grew within me. I was accepted and welcomed. Jesus was within me, and that presence was driving out fear, opening doors and windows to hope and springtime. I would never be alone again.

The transformation was gradual but real. The desire welled up inside me to help others know that they were known and loved; not lost in the crowd, but seen and valued. I wanted my whole life to be about this. And then the draw to become a priest seemed to come from a different place: no longer a form of preordained fate that I was both attracted to and feared, but a powerful flow of love and gratitude that had found its path for expression. I would be a priest. This made sense of 'me' and God in me. I wanted to share what I had received. The call was simple and clear.

When I reflect on the journey described above I recognize it could be a framed as a mystery: Where is the story going? How do we make sense of all the clues? What will be the solution? The mystery is resolved and the story ends. Vocation in this sense is a question awaiting a definitive answer. Life then moves on. But another way of telling your story or mine is the unfolding impact of relationship with God: How does this change us? What do we understand afresh about ourselves or our place in the world? 'Vocation' becomes shorthand for how we go on being drawn out of ourselves in response to a God we encounter through people, places, events and the inward workings of our minds and hearts. Short of death, there can be no ending. A vocational journey might lead a person to the day when they are ordained a priest, but where will it go from there? In a long life a priest will experience many fresh invitations. Like Peter we do not know where the road leads – only who we go with.

A priest seeks to model the perfection of Christ

The identification of a priest with the person of Christ is perhaps most immediately recognized in the Eucharist. There a priest speaks Jesus' words, follows him in giving thanks with bread and wine, before breaking and sharing these gifts. The priest physically stands in the place of Christ. It is a humbling moment. For the priest and poet George Herbert it was also deeply troubling. In his poem 'Aaron', Herbert reflected on his own shortcomings. With his 'defects', 'darkness' and 'passions' he felt ill-dressed to follow in the way of Aaron the priest. But then he remembered he had another 'heart, breast and music' in Christ:

> So holy in my head,
> Perfect and light in my deare breast
> My doctrine tun'd in Christ (who is not dead,
> But lives in me while I do rest)
> Come people; Aaron's drest.[5]

Is it possible for a priest to model the perfection of Christ? For Herbert the answer was both 'no' and 'yes'. The 'no' was a reality always present: a priest is as fallible, fickle and flawed as any other person. The 'yes' expressed the possibility of allowing the light of Christ to flicker into flame through opening oneself to God, in acknowledgement of weakness. The Christ-life can never be claimed as a possession; it can only be received in the moment as gift. 'No' and 'yes' always belong together and must never be separated.

As a child I imagined priests to be perfect. Naive perhaps,

---

[5] George Herbert 1593–1633. There are numerous editions of Herbert's poetry. I have used C. A. Patrides (ed.), 1974, *The English Poems of George Herbert*, London: J. M. Dent & Sons Ltd.

but that was how the Church of the time preferred to project the image. The character of the priest connected to the character of the Church: certain, authoritative, without need for forgiveness, above flaw, and therefore above challenge. That image has crumbled, not least through the emergence of cases of sexual abuse by priests. We live in a time shaped for a more humble expression of Church and priesthood. That is a good thing. I doubt if any priest ever imagines themselves to be perfect – at least, not for long! It's possible that out of fear or insecurity a priest might cover up their fallibility or pretend it is not there. But love, truth and the power to heal and reconcile do not break forth when we wear our perfection as a suit of armour. Humility opens the way.

Perhaps, rather than speak of modelling the perfection of Christ, with all the danger that has of projecting a self-made 'holiness' that majors on authority but lacks love, it is more helpful to think of a priest as one who seeks to model what it is to be a human being open to God, through the grace of Christ and the gift of the Spirit. Rather than claim a place high up on the seating plan, we take the low place. Nothing can be done without God's giving. Rather than hide away weakness, we can own it. All humanity can shine with the glory of God, when in union with Christ we make room for him to enable us to be most human and most ourselves:

Come people; Aaron's drest.

4

Rain for Roots:
The Priest as Disciple

'Let us know, let us press on to know the Lord;
his appearing is as sure as the dawn;
he will come to us like the showers,
like the spring rains that water the earth.'[1]

The prophet Hosea encourages his people to press on to know the
Lord. Here is where rain will come to soak dry earth and refresh weary
lives. As one who has given himself to listening and responding to
God's word for the sake of his people, Hosea has personal experience
of this thirst: 'Let *us* know, let *us* press on' he urges.

Priests who summon others to receive the living waters of the
Spirit also live in continual need of this refreshment. In the chapters
that follow I will explore how priests can open themselves to this fall
of spring rain within the challenges and opportunities of the ministry
they exercise. I begin with considering the life of a priest as a disciple:
one who walks in the company of Jesus, giving attention to his words
and following in the way of his trust through uncertainty.

Chapter 5 will explore different perspectives of the ministry of a
priest: as servant, as minister of communion, as one who celebrates
incarnation and as the herald of good news.

Chapter 6 will draw us deeper into the humanity of a priest. We
all need our places of shelter. Rather than stay remote from us and
from our needs, Jesus calls us friends. As friend he works to reconcile
us to our weakness and to heal our wounds.

Hosea assures us that spring rains will water the earth. His trust
rests not in what we do but in God, whose coming is sure, and whose
desire is always to refresh the dry depths of our lives.

---

[1] Hosea 6.3.

> And he appointed twelve, whom he also named apostles, to be
> with him, and to be sent out to proclaim the message, and to
> have authority to cast our demons.[2]

Four small words easily missed amid the drama of the work to come:
'to be with him'. A priest will relate to many people and be present to
a multitude of responsibilities. It is easy to become so jostled by such
crowds that we lose touch with God. But for the men and women who
responded to Jesus' call, being with him was the heartbeat of their
new life. All that they went on to share flowed from this source:

> We declare to you what was from the beginning, what we have
> heard, what we have seen with our eyes, what we have looked
> at and touched with our hands … this life was revealed, and we
> have seen it and testify to it.[3]

The Gospels are the story of being with Jesus: listening to his teaching,
watching his actions, walking with him along the road, sharing food
together and sleeping by his side. The disciples chose to stay in Jesus'
company and to meet the challenge of all this would mean in terms
of personal conversion. As a teenager, reading the New Testament
for the first time, this is what I wanted: to be seen amid the crowd,
called forward, and invited to live in Jesus' presence. Previously I had
thought that being a Christian was summed up by believing in God
and maintaining high standards of moral behaviour. Now I began to
understand: beyond following Jesus by means of my behaviour and
attitudes, I was invited to be with him, and to enjoy his being with me.

Our first glimpse of Jesus in the Gospel of John is through the
eyes of John the Baptist and two of his disciples. John recognized the
one he had been waiting for and pointed him out as the Lamb of God
come to take away the sin of the world. Hearing these words, John's
disciples followed Jesus as he walked by. Turning, he asked them
what they were looking for. They answered, 'Rabbi, where are you
staying?' 'Come and see,' Jesus replied. They went with him and saw

---

[2] Mark 3.14–15.
[3] 1 John 1.1–2.

where he was staying, and 'remained with him that day'.[4] Here – with hospitality – their story begins and will continue. Deeds will follow: good news will be preached; lives will be healed. But the grounding for their ministry will always be this homely intimacy: 'Come and see where I live ... remain with me.'

Later in John's Gospel the message becomes more explicit:

'Abide in me as I abide in you ... Those who abide in me and I in them bear much fruit, because apart from me you can do nothing.'[5]

The message is clear: outside this abiding nothing can be done; no fruit can be borne. It is worth pausing here to take that in. There is a fundamental choice to make as to where we rest our life. We tend to think of discipleship in terms of things we do, but it begins and continues in the choice to 'be with'. I still forget this, plunging onwards in doing things for God until I become as empty as my words. Then, even as I fall apart, the invitation comes again in all its startling simplicity: 'Come and see where I live.' The door is always open and the table is laid. In times to come the disciples will be sent to the ends of the Earth; but they will never be far from home. 'I am with you always,'[6] Jesus promises, 'abide in me'.

Our life in God rests not in something we do but in what is given. God has chosen us as dwelling place and is at home within. Jesus says, 'I abide in you'. In the Gospels we see this choice expressed physically in Jesus sitting down to eat with those labelled by others as tax collectors and sinners. Just as with our clothes, labels have a habit of sticking out so all can see them; but the God who knows our names has no use for identification tags. God is at home with who you are. God is at home with you even though you are not yet at home with yourself. Priests are as much in need of this gospel as anyone else. Everything begins and goes on from here. God's choice is made; our choice is before us: 'come and see where I live; remain with me'.

God's simplicity confounds us. We want to complicate the relationship by seeking to earn our place in the household. As a priest

---

[4] John 1.35–42.
[5] John 15.4–5.
[6] Matthew 28.20.

I did not fully understand my significance to God. I easily lapsed into the work ethic that had defined my life with its simple mathematical equations: worth comes from what I do; another's acceptance of you must be earned. God does not understand such 'money talk'. God's choices are not determined by our responses. Our creeds proclaim that in an intersection of time and space God pitched his tent among us, to reveal that always and everywhere God chooses to be in our company. Like the two sons of a prodigal father we do not understand our place in the household. Some seek their identity elsewhere, and others live as outsiders in the house intended to be their home. For tax collectors and sinners, scribes and Pharisees, the challenge is one and the same: choose as your resting place the God who freely chooses to be at rest in you. There you will discover who you are and how to live.

Intimacy within any relationship brings challenges. Two lives will distantly pass each other by in the absence of a mutual commitment to be in one another's company. Closeness requires a degree of openness that can make us feel vulnerable. It is often difficult to let down our defences and allow another in when our house is untidy and in need of repair. But this other is already at home, waiting for us to find him there by going deep within. Perhaps it is better to keep things at a safe level – no more than a nodding acquaintance. That way we can keep things under our control; nothing has to change. Jesus rarely left undisturbed the lives of those he met unless they chose to avoid his gaze and discount his words. He condemned the religious leaders of his time for the personal convenience of their religious practice and the impact this had on those under their care:

> 'But woe to you, scribes and Pharisees, hypocrites! For you lock people out of the kingdom of heaven. For you do not go in yourselves, and when others are going in, you stop them.'[7]

Here too is the importance of our 'going in'; without this – even without wishing it – we can begin to stand in the way of those who are seeking to find their home in God. The ministry of a priest can provide the door that helps another connect their experience with the presence and working of the Spirit. But this door can also remain tight shut. What do people experience in the company of a priest? What do

[7] Matthew 23.13–14.

they see, hear and sense about what moves this person to be as they are? Does the encounter draw them towards depth of relationship with God or does it drive them away? What attracts and invites is not the priest's perfection, but the sense of their intimacy with God. Does their life seem to flow from a dependence on God's giving? Do they seem at home with who they are in being less than perfect, in a way that enables another to be at home in their company?

Being with: A way of life

> Surely goodness and mercy shall follow me
>   all the days of my life,
> and I shall dwell in the house of the Lord
>   my whole life long.[8]

Psalm 23 is almost too familiar to be surprised by its words; but it bears a lifetime's pondering and living. To awake to what it holds, it might help to begin in a different place: at its ending. Though there is continual movement through the psalm, leading us by still waters and through dark valleys, the writer knows he never leaves home. He travels amid danger and delight and is always in the house of the Lord. For any disciple and any priest, stuff happens: the welcomed and unwanted, the setbacks and the breakthroughs. There are days of darkness and pain, and days of wonder and gratitude. Within – rather than despite – this tumult of thoughts, feelings and events, goodness and mercy follow us. It is not that all that happens to us is good, but the Good One is with us through all that happens. 'Being with' is our home, and the door is always open. 'Being with' is not an escape from reality but the way to meet reality without it overwhelming us. In the midst of enemies a table is spread and the cup overflows. We follow one who leads us to unlikely green pastures and surprising still waters, and everywhere we are followed by goodness and mercy.

There is a moment in the psalm when what is said in the third person for the hearing of others is not enough. The psalmist cries out: '*You* are with me ... *you* prepare a table before me ... *you* anoint my head with oil.'[9] This is not theory; it is experience of togetherness

---

[8] Psalm 23.6.
[9] Psalm 23.5.

where the only fitting language is that of 'I' and 'You'. There is part of me that has often resisted such intimacy with God, even as I have longed for it. I doubt that I have such significance. It is no small thing to rest in the belief that, as we are, God wants us, chooses us and makes home with us. And here I need to take away that generalized 'we': I mean 'I'; I mean 'you'. I wonder if this is what prevents many people and many priests going deeper in relationship with God: at depth we do not believe God could be that personally interested in us or have such an intense longing that we find our home in goodness and mercy. God is good … but not *that* good. Here is where the leap comes in. Though we might not feel nor believe that God invites us, we must choose to act as if it were so. Dismissing or sidestepping our objections, we decide to enter the house of the Lord as if there really was a place laid out that belongs to us alone. As we persist in doing so we become more comfortable with God's intimacy with us; it gets easier to cross the threshold. We begin to trust that we do belong.

Entering the house of the Lord

> 'You will know that I am in my Father, and you in me, and I in you.'[10]

We enter by invitation; and this invitation extends to all rather than to a select few. We enter by actively choosing to 'be with' God in response to God's choice to abide with us. I have avoided using the word 'prayer' until this point, even though it properly belongs to any consideration of the lived experience of being in relationship with God. 'Prayer' is a good word, but for some it has unhelpful associations:

- Prayer is for those who have mastered the right technique.
- There are praying people and active people.
- Prayer 'works' when the one who prays has a direct and continuous experience of the presence of God.
- Prayer has a particular set form (which might be one that has never worked for me).

Keeping it simple, prayer is what takes place when someone chooses to be with God. While there is a great deal of helpful guidance about

---

[10] John 14.20.

how we can become more focused and open within different forms of prayer, prayer happens the moment we turn our attention towards God, even when our efforts feel haphazard and clumsy. Sometimes we are aware of God as we pray and sometimes not; if our desire seeks God that is enough, whatever the results might be. There are many different ways to actively choose to be with God and abide in that company; it is always possible to find means of prayer that work with our particular personality and circumstances. There is room for all in the house of the Lord. God has no favourites, and everyone is a favourite. Just as different personalities found themselves welcomed in Jesus' company, there is a place for each of us. Peter with his 'act first, think later' approach to life has an equal place with the reflective John, the busy Martha, the questioning Thomas and the physically expressive Mary of Bethany. The decisive factor in each of these lives was their choice to be with Jesus; all else was secondary to this. You can be yourself and be with God.

Through a limited understanding of prayer, or an underestimation of how much God desires our active company, it might be that we have never explored our place within the house of the Lord. We hang around the threshold, without moving entirely away or fully entering in. Perhaps this might be the day when, like Zacchaeus, Jesus sees us at the back of the crowd, enviously observing other people's intimacy, and tells us to 'hurry and come down, for I must stay at your house today'.[11] Or, like the woman with a haemorrhage, we dare to push through the crowd as if we had a place at Jesus' side.[12] Prayer is a choice to believe in God's active hope at work for us, even when our trained mind tells us our belief is ill-founded. There is discipline involved in the choice to pray. The discipline is on our side, moving against our inward detractors that tell us we are of small account to God. The discipline is also on the side of God, persistently choosing to draw us into the relationship that alone can integrate our scattered being and make our activity fruitful. Discipline in this sense is not punishment or burden, but the free expression of desire that also leads to our release. The way still has to be chosen; discipline expresses the path of a disciple. We make a decision, and renew it each day, to be

[11] Luke 19.5.
[12] Mark 5.25–34.

with the one who has chosen to make home with us. Prayer is not one more 'ought' we feel bad about for not achieving; it is allowing God the room to go on liberating us into the active expression of our individuality, in ways that are life-giving for others. For Peter, Martha, John, Thomas and Mary this was what being with Jesus was about; each day a new adventure in their becoming.

The way of a disciple is expressed in these heartfelt words of Jesus:

> 'Come to me, all you that are weary and are carrying heavy burdens, and I will give you rest. Take my yoke upon you, and learn from me; for I am gentle and humble in heart, and you will find rest for your souls. For my yoke is easy, and my burden is light.'[13]

Like Psalm 23 the words are so familiar we stop hearing them; or – and this is a particular tendency for priests – we hear and speak them for other people without allowing them to rest first with us. So hear and receive the invitation: 'Come to me'. The words echo those spoken by Jesus to the disciples of John the Baptist: 'Come and see'. The gift that awaits us is rest. This rest is more than the pause between work and more work; it is our resting place amid activity. The yoke of the disciple is the one Jesus shares: to make relationship with God our default place of belonging. Though there is a burden of discipline upon us of responding afresh to God's invitation, when we do so, the weight of our living and working eases. The words of Jesus leap time and place to address you and I, 'Come … and you will find rest for your souls.'

Prayer as the way of abiding

> 'Those who love me will keep my word, and my Father will love them, and we will come to them and make our home with them.'[14]

Teresa of Avila was a woman of action. In the face of considerable opposition she set about the reform of the Carmelite community, returning to its founding principles of simplicity of life, deepening

---

[13] Matthew 11.28–30.
[14] John 14.23.

prayer, humble self-awareness and generosity of heart. Teresa travelled across Spain setting up new communities, writing endless letters of advice and spiritual guidance. She persisted in ploughing a way through the inertia of Church bureaucracy to fulfil the vision she understood God had given her. She was a 'doer'; and she was also a contemplative woman of prayer.

For many years the relationship between prayer and activity was uppermost in her mind. In her earlier life, some of her experiences of prayer were so overwhelming that she felt unable in that moment to do anything. Being absorbed in God seemed to allow no room to be taken up with people or with work that required her attention. As an older woman her understanding of what it was to be with God through prayer evolved. Where once she assumed full union with God through prayer was so powerful an experience that it made any activity impossible, now she understood oneness with God as a quiet awareness of inward presence. The words of Jesus in the Gospel of John came alive for her. She sensed the company of the Trinity within, as if in an inner room, not as occasional guests but as those who have made their lifelong home there. Rather than preventing her activity, this presence inspired it. Speaking about herself she concluded, 'it seemed to her, despite the trials she underwent and the business affairs she had to attend to, that the essential part of her soul never moved from that room'.[15] Her home was in the Trinity's home within her. She could be active and yet 'be with'. Such a union of prayer and activity was not easily won. Writing about the discipline of choosing to be in God's company she described the challenge of becoming accustomed to 'caring nothing at all about seeing or hearing, to practising the hours of prayer, and thus to solitude and withdrawal'.[16] For the disciple, there is discipline. There are other homes we might choose rather than this one. We can lose ourselves in activity. There is always necessary work to be done. But whose work is it? The choice is not between prayer and activity, but between making the source of

---

[15] Kieran Kavanagh and Otilio Rodriguez, 1980, *The Collected Works of Teresa of Avila*, Washington DC: ICS Publications, Volume Two, 'The Interior Castle' 7:1.10.

[16] Kavanagh and Rodriguez, *The Collected Works of Teresa of Avila*, Volume One, 'The Book of Her Life' 11.9.

that activity our own driveness, and allowing activity to flow from a place of rest in God.

I find the image of an inner room a helpful one. In the midst of activity I can step inside. Beginning any work I can start from my place in the room of indwelling, and as Teresa shows me, I can stay in that room even as I work. For this to become a reality I have to become used to choosing this room as my dwelling place. I seek God, who seeks me. I turn to God whose face is always turned to me. Once more I make my home in God, who has long made home in me.

Be with me

It is time to put aside questions as to whether or not we are good at prayer, natural contemplatives or people of action. These are more labels God doesn't see. God simply says: 'Come'. All that matters is that we respond; and it is vital that we do so for our own spiritual wellbeing, and for that of people whose lives we touch.

How we respond will vary with who we are and the circumstances in which we live and work. For all there will be some regular and chosen time. Any relationship rests on this. In a marriage as much as a religious vocation some discipline is needed. Two people might be crossing paths or sharing space for a good portion of the day, but if they are not to take each other for granted and allow their love to grow cold, both must actively choose to set aside time where there is no other focus than being together. It takes work. Nearness and familiarity tend to invite laziness in treasuring and nurturing the relationship. A priest might be around the things of God all day but there is still a need for chosen time when other business is set aside for the sake of consciously being with one another. God goes on making this choice, and waits for us to do the same.

Talk of discipline is not easy if by nature we are someone inclined to be free from restrictions, walking our own path. This, however, is the very point about discipleship: the decisions we make and the actions that flow from them are to be chosen, not imposed. When we begin to think of prayer as a burdensome task it helps to choose it, all over again. At one point in John's Gospel, Jesus' followers walk away because they cannot deal with what he says. They are free to do so. Jesus turns to those closest to him and asks, 'Do you also wish to go away?' Peter responds, 'Lord, to whom can we go? You have the words of eternal life.'[17] What will we choose? God does not demand our obedience; God awaits our free response.

For those people with a natural gift for planning the day and ordering time, setting aside a regular time for prayer is likely to come easily. But what if you a person who lives by spontaneity and variety of pattern? Without being absolute about it, some constancy of practice will still prove helpful. 'Habit' can have negative associations: a person repeats what they do and their mind or heart might or might not be in it. It is possible to become stuck in ways of acting or being that are less than helpful. But growing into a habit of behaviour can also work for a change of direction we desire to take. With repetition it becomes easier to stay with the action that expresses the desire of the heart without endless inner debate about whether there is something more useful or enjoyable we might be doing with our time. I get up in the morning and I make tea; it is what my mind and body needs. I do not spend a lot of time considering what other beverage I might require or whether I should do press ups before I put the kettle on. We can speak dismissively of 'going through the motions' when action appears not to be thought through in the moment. But before we discard the 'motions' in favour of the purity of the inner spirit it helps to remember we are bodily people; physical actions can help make our spirit ready. This is certainly true when it come to prayer. Choosing a regular place, time, posture, and way of beginning and ending our prayer can provide a supportive framework for developing our openness to God.

Place

Make a particular room, or seat, or walking route a habitual place for prayer. Of course we can pray anywhere. But through repetition the mind and spirit begin to recognize that in entering *this* place I am setting myself to pray. Priests generally have privileged access to a church. Your place of being with God doesn't have to be there – but it could be. It might help to choose your own space within the church as your regular place of meeting: a particular pew or a side chapel. When you sit in that place you know why you are there. Your 'place' might

---

[17] John 6.68.

equally be your kitchen table at a quiet time of the day, or a certain bench in the garden. A regular walk can also become a conscious and chosen time of 'being with'. This walk is not just movement from A to B; you choose to walk in step with God, being alive to what is around you. You also open yourself to how all things lead you into God and God into you.

Greeting

Familiar words or gestures can help us acknowledge that we have entered God's presence. This might be the lighting of a candle, the bowing before a cross, or saying a particular prayer or a verse from one of the psalms. Regular usage helps us move more quickly into prayer. We understand we are here for this purpose and for no other.

Posture

I remember being taught at school how to set the body for prayer: eyes closed and hands together. Then a particular posture for prayer was not an option – it was a requirement. Nowadays I usually pray with open eyes. But there is wisdom in using the body to help the mind into a place of prayer: for example, sitting with hands open and resting on our laps or, if walking, a slower, measured pace that begins to settle us down. As these physical settings become familiar, our spirit begins to work in unison, helping us be relaxed, open and attentive.

Time

Here there are two considerations: time of day and length of time spent in prayer. There is no right and wrong as to whether we find a more extended time of prayer in the morning, afternoon, evening or night. What will help is to settle on a time that we can usually count on as being ours (and when we are likely to be awake!). Jesus seemed to find that time in the early hours of the morning, but that will not work for all of us. When our chosen time of the day comes around we know what it is for. Given that the unexpected might be the ordinary movement of the day, there may be times when we have to forego this pause with God, with the hope that we might find it later; but do not let it go too easily. Be wary of that worm of a thought that suggests there are more important things to do than waste time with God.

As to length of time we spend in consciously being with God, fixing on a period and staying with it is perhaps as important as duration. If it is half an hour, then abide for that half an hour, even if nothing much seems to be happening. What is taking place is meeting, though from our side it might seem we are no more than a bundle of distractions. God works within that room we make whether we are aware of it or not.

Ending and moving on

Just as we have greeted God at the beginning of prayer, so we choose a way of closing this time, while remaining open to God's presence as we go about our day. Again this might be a physical action such as the sign of the cross or blowing out a candle, words of a prayer or a verse from the psalms.

Being with God in the midst of activity

A chosen time of being with God sensitizes us to how we are never apart: everywhere we go we find ourselves on holy ground. Or as the writer of Psalm 23 expresses it, goodness and mercy follow us always, and even though we travel far, we remain in the house of the Lord. Many people today – within and outside faith communities – find refuge and balance in the practice of mindfulness. When we are mindful, we are wholly in the present. The past and future sweep in and out of our consciousness; we allow them free passage without moving with them out of the moment. Our thoughts and feelings come in judgement of ourselves and others; we own them but do not hold on to them. What matters is 'here' and 'now'. We release our need to be the centre of the world, and become open to what is before us without shaping it with our agendas, fears, desires or drives. From a Christian perspective this being in the here and now is also 'being with'. There is presence in the present: a presence that sometimes makes us cry out with wonder or raise heart and mind in thanksgiving. This awareness of God-breathed reality will be developed in the chapters to come but for the moment note the continuity between being with God and being with all that a day brings. In abiding in the moment we also abide in God, as God abides in us. Even as we listen to another, hold a lengthy and frustrating meeting or check out the building work in the church, we are in the house of the Lord. With those first disciples we walk in Jesus' company, sit by his side and share his bread.

A word for the uncertain

I look at a cookery programme and hear the presenter saying this recipe is so simple that anyone could make it. I hear an IT specialist telling me how straightforward it is to change this or that setting on my computer. I want to believe them, but don't. It might be that simple, but I hold myself back from trying through lack of confidence. Perhaps it might be the same for you with prayer. But before you draw away here are some things to remember:

God abides in you
Prayer is not a way we make God happen through the intensity of our focus and our determination to eliminate distractions. God is already there. As we choose to abide in God our life begins to flow from this source.

You are significant to God
God wants to make you whole and complete. God desires to be with you and for you to find your home in this relationship. There are many in the crowd, but you are the one Jesus notices and calls.

God made you who you are
Your personality is not a barrier in God's eyes; it is a chosen door God desires to move through. God is at home with who you are, and in this, you have the foundation to be at home with yourself and become a home for others.

In the end, everything is gift
Prayer is cooperation with the Spirit's moving. While we do make an active choice to set ourselves in a place of prayer, it is the Spirit who prays in us – even through our hesitations and distractions. We give our attention but also relax. Prayer is not another thing to achieve by sheer grit and determination, or perfection of technique. In the end, everything is gift.

Dweller with the Word

The Lord God has given me the tongue of a teacher,
that I may know how to sustain the weary with a word.
Morning by morning he wakens – wakens my ear
to listen as those who are taught.[18]

A priest needs both the tongue of a teacher and the ear of a listener. The weary need a word; but what to say? The word comes to those who listen; the teacher must first be taught. Through a stance of wakeful awareness the teacher receives the word for the weary.

A priest is a teacher, and also a disciple. They too need a word for their weariness. Outside of being a disciple a priest has nothing of value to say. Though there are many words that describe the foundational beliefs of the Church, and others of moral guidance, outside the lived experience of being a disciple such words remain dust. The words that give life are more than combinations of symbols and sounds; they flow from relationship; they emerge into being through the struggle to keep listening and responding to the one who meets us in all things:

> The word of God is living and active, sharper than any two-edged sword, piercing until it divides soul from spirit, joints from marrow; it is able to judge the thoughts and intentions of the heart. And before him no creature is hidden, but all are naked and laid bare to the eyes of the one to whom we must render an account.[19]

The word is not tame, safe or 'ours'; to receive it is to be challenged. The word is also the creative movement of God into our universe and into our lives. The word is Scripture and it is more than Scripture; the word is the experience of our lives and also transcends this experience. When the word is made flesh, lives are changed, because the word is the one who is life. To receive the word requires silence: not the silence of absence of sounds but the silence of naked, laid-bare attentiveness.

---

18 Isaiah 50.4.
19 Hebrews 4.12–13.

A priest is a teacher and preacher, and always a disciple. No amount of training and formation at theological college or seminary can provide the necessary words for this day, in this place, and for these people. The activity of breaking open the word depends on the contemplative practice of being before God with our experience and pondering its significance in humble awareness of our dependence on the Spirit, our guide and teacher. But how realistic is it to be contemplative within such a demanding and active life?

Joining the Gospel dots

The figures of Martha and Mary have almost become cast in stone as stereotypes. Martha is busy about many things; Mary sits before Jesus' feet. Martha is distracted by her anxious – and sometimes resentful – thoughts; Mary chooses the simplicity of the one necessary thing: to be attentive to what is taking place in the moment.[20] While many priests – male and female – might aspire to sit with Mary, most find themselves driven to be alongside Martha in the kitchen: there are people to be fed after all. Luke's inclusion of this intimate, domestic moment has a more nuanced purpose than we might suppose. Immediately preceding the meal in Bethany, a teacher challenges Jesus to name what leads to eternal life. Jesus tells the story of a man left for dead on the road to Jericho. A priest and a Levite pass by; but a Samaritan stops to tend the wounded man and takes him to an inn where he can be looked after. 'Go and do likewise,' says Jesus.[21] Active care is necessary. What joins the two stories is not so much the need to stop doing, as the primary place of attentiveness. What the moment requires is to let go of all previous agendas and be present to what is taking place here and now. For the most part Martha has it right; she sees the weariness on the face of the travelling teacher and welcomes him into her home.

Historically the story of Martha and Mary has been used to classify people as either active or contemplative, but as tempting as it might be to do this, it won't do. Attentiveness joins the Gospel dots: in being open to God met in all our experience, we see what needs

[20] Luke 10.38–42.
[21] Luke 10.25–37.

to be done and we gain the generosity of heart to do it. Attentiveness cannot be shortcut; it requires a deliberate choice not to be so lost in activity that we stop being in relationship with the one who addresses us in all things. Contemplation will always lead us into active care for the other: the more we are present to God, the more we will find ourselves carried outwards in the flow of God's creative love.

Once upon a Saturday afternoon I was preparing a homily for the coming evening on the story of the Good Samaritan. What my 'preparing' amounted to was some fretful and unproductive scratching around looking for something fresh to say about such a familiar tale. The pressure was mounting. Then the doorbell rang. A homeless man was there – what a time to choose! My impatience rose. I fixed him a sandwich and a cup of tea and he went on his way. I bent my thoughts back to my task: still no inspiration. The doorbell rang again; someone wanted to talk. The words formed in my mind: 'This is a really bad time. I can't see you at the moment; if you come back on Monday … I have to prepare this sermon on the Good Samaritan and I can't think what to say.' It took that long for me to begin to notice the big log stuck in my eye. God had given me a story to share; it was time to laugh at my own expense, and give my attention to the one who had brought the word to me.

Look and learn

My parents left school aged 14. They wanted more for their children. So while I was given free rein to read the *Beano* or the *Beezer*, I was also expected to read *Look and Learn*. The title tells you all: this was an educational magazine, full of useful facts about the world accompanied by drawings to fire the imagination. I loved it. Jesus was also of the 'look and learn' persuasion:

> 'Consider the ravens; they neither sow nor reap, they have neither storehouse nor barn, and yet God feeds them.'[22]

> 'Look around you, and see how the fields are ripe for harvesting.'[23]

---

[22] Luke 12.24.
[23] John 4.35.

'Listen! A sower went out to sow.'[24]

'Be alert at all times.'[25]

'And what I say to you I say to all: Keep awake.'[26]

Jesus' own teaching reveals a contemplative awareness of the wonders hidden within daily experience: a farmer sowing seeds, a merchant seeking the finest of pearls, a woman who sweeps her house in search of a lost coin. Lost in the forest of events, we might not notice the trees that surround us: 'Listen, look, stay awake!' Through the active practice of being present to the moment – the beating heart, the pattern of clouds, the person we are with or the feel of our foot on the ground – we begin to be alive to life itself. The exercise of such awareness is both active and passive. It is active because we choose to rest our gaze here, and to listen with the intent of hearing and understanding. It is passive because we are also consenting to be in relationship with what or who is before us: we have to let go of imposing our own agendas or packing what we receive into our pre-formed boxes. This is the essence of the contemplative way. In stilling ourselves to become alive to what is 'here' and 'now', we become open to God, the I AM who fills this and every moment. The present is full of presence.

We all have the capacity for contemplation. Imagine yourself eating the most delicious of food and savouring each mouthful; or remember a time when the beauty of a piece of music held all your attention; place yourself afresh within the memory of watching waves fall on the beach or a small child at play. For a brief time nothing else matters or exists; what is before you is enough. In that moment you are a contemplative. One simple way of developing the practice of contemplation is choosing to spend five minutes each day being present with one or more of your senses to where you are: the colours of the sky, the feeling of the sun on your back, the movement of tree branches in the wind or the sounds of a city street. It might be said – and with justification – that practising presence in this way is not

---

[24] Mark 4.3.
[25] Luke 21.36.
[26] Mark 13.37.

in itself a form of prayer; and yet, it easily becomes prayer with the simple acknowledgement that in this moment we are with God and God is with us. A 'thank you' turns our awareness into gratitude for relationship.

Why does developing our capacity for contemplation matter for priests in particular? Because priests are ministers of relationship – of God met in all things. Because the attentiveness of contemplation is also the attentiveness they bring into any pastoral situation. It takes care and attention to be sensitive to what is happening for others and to communicate an active presence that enables them to feel heard and valued. The Jesus who is alive to the birds of the sky and the ways of the fishermen is also the Jesus who notices the one at the back of the crowd who, of all present, most needs healing. It is through the practice of contemplation that the word for the weary is heard. The practice of contemplation also makes us happier and removes our sense of isolation; we become aware of the great gift of simple things, and the Giver who desires to make our lives complete. This is the gospel a priest proclaims.

The reality of priestly ministry is often a great deal of necessary activity and very little predictability about the pattern of each day. This might seem to place significant obstacles to living contemplatively in any meaningful way. Time is disrupted; there are no wide oceans of silence to invite us into simple presence to presence. Rather than abandon the attempt to live attentively it is good to explore and experiment with practices of contemplation that might – with a little determination – prove sustainable. Five minutes of sensing will always be possible, even if not always at the same time of the day. Sometimes the flow of the day will allow the five minutes to become ten; it is helpful to be generous with ourselves and God as events allow; but guard that precious five minutes. For many years I have found walking a place of gentle encounter with God. Without working too hard at it, I look to let go of active thoughts and be present to where I am and what I am passing. Thoughts do come – in great rushes sometimes – but rather than catch their hook and allow them to drag me around, I allow them to come and go. I am not actively thinking about God, but I am quietly aware of God with me. Sometimes conversation with God breaks out, and this too becomes part of the flow. For a moment I might stop walking and take in where I am more fully, and then my steps renew. A friend of mine finds time within the busyness of the day to knit – ten minutes here and another ten minutes there. As he knits, the rhythm of repetitive movement begins to unravel the tangle of thoughts, feelings and obligations. It is enough to be present to the wool and the needles: God is there too. Perhaps if you live in a city you might go to an art gallery and place yourself before one painting – and one painting only. Gaze at what is before you, and allow the image to look back at you. What might work for you? Perhaps you will only discover this if you persist with exploration. Don't jump from one practice to another. Choose one and keep with it long enough for it to begin to become habitual. You may have to stay with it through the times when everything tells you it's not working for it to begin its transforming work with you.

I am aware I am using the word 'contemplation' loosely and there are more formal patterns of prayer that give the practice more definite shape and form. Centring prayer and Christian meditation have roots that go down to the early Christian centuries. Both seek to deepen our receptivity to God by loosening our attachment to self-generated agendas and thoughts. What more important thing can there be for a priest to learn than to make this movement? It is as if we become a hollow in the ground where the falling rain gathers to provide drink for those who are thirsty. And we too are being refreshed, though outwardly we may know little about it.

Noticing

> The word that came to Jeremiah from the Lord: 'Come, go down to the potter's house, and there I will let you hear my words.' So I went down to the potter's house, and there he was working at his wheel. The vessel he was making of clay was spoiled in the potter's hand, and he reworked it into another vessel, as seemed good to him. Then the word of the Lord came to me: 'Can I not do with you, O house of Israel, just as this potter has done?'[27]

How does the 'word of the Lord' come? There may be many doors through which it makes entry; most of them belong to the ordinary,

[27] Jeremiah 18.1–6.

rather than dramatic visual or aural experience. How did Jeremiah receive his instruction to go to the potter's house? I wonder if it was neither more nor less than an inward draw, akin to the way you might one day find yourself choosing to walk down a particular street or to ring a particular person. You can't explain in any clear terms why you are doing so; it seems in that moment the thing to do. Jeremiah goes into the potter's house, and you walk down your street or make your phone call. Inside the house, Jeremiah is taken up with watching the potter at work. Is this what a prophet does? Shouldn't he be preparing his latest oration? Time passes. The clay rises in the potter's hand, but not being perfect he brings it down again to reform its shape. Jeremiah notices that particular movement; the wet clay being as pliable as it is, this rising and falling in the potter's hand happens more than once. Then Jeremiah understands: the people are as clay in the hands of the Lord. The word of the Lord came to Jeremiah; or was it that the word of the Lord had been coming to Jeremiah since he first noticed and followed that inexplicable urge to visit the house of the potter?

Receiving the word depends on noticing. The significant movement is usually small and easily missed. Often the meaning of what is seen, heard or sensed is not immediately apparent. But as the experience is held, pondered and waited upon, understanding begins to seep through. The word unfolds as much by passive receptiveness as active reflection; it comes by gift and not just force of mental process.

A priest is called to dwell with the word in this way: to daily ponder the Scriptures and experience. The appropriate stance is that of Jeremiah: noticing the nudges; staying with what is heard or seen; allowing time – and God – to take us deeper into what has been received. Two practices in particular express this patient process of attending to the word: the prayerful reading of Scripture (*lectio divina*) and daily remembering the day with God (*the examen*). The *examen* has a further dimension of discernment, and for that reason I will explore its use within the section on the priest as pilgrim traveller, where choice of path becomes vital, but the two practices remain cousins. At their heart is attentiveness to what is being revealed through our experience as we dwell in the presence of God.

Lectio divina

The theory and practice of *lectio divina* are probably familiar. Below I will briefly rehearse them; you will find fuller treatments elsewhere. My purposes here are in the first place to underline the unifying stance of the different movements of the exercise, and also to explore how priests might use it given the wide variety of Scripture they encounter in the natural course of their ministry.

Lectio (reading / hearing)

We 'hear' the Scripture reading. This implies more than simply reading the words – as we might with a newspaper or book. This is a relational exercise: we begin and continue in the presence of a God who is always reaching out to us, and is doing so now through these words. We listen out for words, phrases or images that seem to touch us – perhaps as obliquely as Jeremiah's nudge to visit the potter's house. The movement is one of noticing – or of being guided to notice.

Meditatio (pondering)

Remaining in the presence of God, we ponder those words and any linked images or feelings that seem to be for us today. It may help to read through the words again. Pondering suggests the active use of our minds. With Jeremiah we begin to enquire why it is we notice these words or have this inner response. Our attention becomes more deeply focused on what has moved us. While our minds are actively engaged, this is more than a mental puzzle awaiting a solution that lies within the power of our reach: we must remain open, for it is the Spirit that is our guide and teacher here. 'Pondering' suggests this stance of active, yet patient attentiveness.

Oratio (responding)

As meaning unfolds we respond to how God meets us in these words. How am I called, challenged, invited or comforted by God present to me now? Our response may take the form of words, or be made in some other way – perhaps by a physical expression of how we feel or what we need.

Contemplatio (resting)

Here it is enough to be with God who reaches out to us in this way. Thoughts and feelings are there, but less actively pursued. We rest as God continues to work for us, taking us deeper into what we have received. The temptation might be to move along quickly; we have got our word for the day, what else do we need? Imagine someone watering plants in dry ground: it is not enough to make the ground wet; the water must continue to flow until it reaches down to the deepest roots. So we abide here while the gardener does his work.

Lectio divina is naturally aligned with the life and work of a priest. With the daily Office and readings set for the Eucharist there is no shortage of biblical material to work on. This in itself can create a challenge: how possible is it to consider Scripture in depth when each day provides so much of it? The answer is short and clear: it is not possible! So for this exercise, focus on one thing: this might be the daily Gospel given for the Eucharist or one of the psalms provided for morning or evening prayer. As you hear or read your selected passage listen out for the words or the phrase that wake afresh for you; centre your attention here. You are sifting through words seeking God's word for you on this day; you are allowing God to lead you to the place where your attention is to rest.

Lectio divina is a valued practice for priests not so much for the details of its different movements as for the stance towards scripture it expresses. This living word of God continually invites us into relationship. There is great value in the study of Scripture: we see more through its words and stories as a result. But *lectio divina* asks something more of us: to be open and attentive before God who desires to lead us beyond where we now stand. We use all we have at our disposal: our will to set aside the time, our minds to ponder what we hear, our openness and courage to allow ourselves to be surprised, comforted and disturbed by the words that are given. We also need the humility to let go into God and consent to being guided and led. This stance belongs not just to receiving the word of God in Scripture but the word of God spoken in daily life. *Lectio divina* sharpens the tools we bring to being attentive and responsive to God met in all things – even a potter moulding wet clay into the vessel he desires.

Breaking and sharing the bread of the word

The task of breaking open and sharing the word of God through teaching and preaching provides both opportunity and danger for a priest. Opportunity: because it provides a compelling reason for sitting with the Scriptures and pondering their significance. Danger: because if we are not careful, dwelling with Scripture can be reduced to seeking a product to share without allowing it to touch the sides of our own experience. The words and stories of the Bible always address us first.

I welcomed the daily Eucharist as a helpful prod encouraging me to dwell with the word of God in Scripture. I felt it important to suggest some way in which the given words of the readings of the day touched everyday experience. I wasn't (I don't think) in love with the sound of my own voice. I understood that this word, however outwardly obscure, had something to say to my life – and then beyond me to the lives of those gathered to hear it. I wouldn't know what this was until I sat with it. I had to use my mind but also be receptive. The process wasn't as simple as working out the meaning, the way one might approach a mental puzzle that has one correct solution. The word was not my creature, tamed and obedient; it needed room – my room – to be free to roam through the events of the day and the ways the world had been turning, before I could begin to receive what it had to say. Perhaps it might be no more than a single line of meaning worth sharing: my word, but also a word that was beyond me.

Every priest who wrestles with the task of preaching has their own process, but the outline of what I have described might feel familiar. The preacher works with the word of God, and the word of God works with the preacher. The personality, personal history and circumstances of the priest are not left behind, and they are also not the sum total of what is shared. Let me suggest another picture. Imagine I have a mixing bowl in my hand. Into it I pour the words of Scripture provided for the day. Then I add all I have been hearing, seeing and feeling. I stir in the experience of those I have listened to or worked with. I sift in what is happening in the wider world and how this seems to touch our lives. I mix together all that is in the bowl. I don't know for sure what it is that I am involved in creating – only that it is food to be shared. Now and again I stir as seems needful, but as with most recipes there is a good deal of waiting.

There are skills that can be acquired to enable preaching to be more effective. Most priests will have memories of preaching workshops and painful feedback. But below this icing lies the cake: making oneself open to dwell with the word of God spoken in scripture and in life. The one who speaks has first to listen – and listen well.

What does this contemplative stance towards experience and revelation look like in practice? A person who comes to mind is Julian of Norwich. She was an anchoress rather than a priest, so why look at her example? For me Julian holds together being a pastor, a theologian, a teacher and a person of prayer – and this to me seems to express the responsibility and privilege of a priest. Julian listened to people's experiences on the smaller and larger scale. She would have heard news of the distressing events of her time: failed harvests, wars with France, plague, the ruthless putting down of revolts by people of the land seeking freedom from feudal oppression. She also took to herself the experiences of those who sought her counsel and prayer: birth, death, loss, bewilderment, choices to be made and questions awaiting answers. She brought to her contemplation of these things her own experience of the persistent and generous love of God. She was a loyal daughter of the Church who received but also wrestled with aspects of its teaching. Large in Julian's life were questions awoken by the pain of others: Why does a good and loving God allow such destructiveness to happen? Where is God within our struggling? In her prayer Julian held all these things, and from her prayer emerged words that she understood were meant for her, but also for the comfort and guidance of others. What gives Julian's words such authenticity and relevance for our time – even though 600 years have passed since her death – was her willingness to be the mixing bowl. She was willing to hear all things, receive all pains, allow all questions, while resting in the depths of her relationship with God. She desired words of life for others and chose to stay in the listening place long enough for these to emerge. For Julian, theology concerned life: God's life, her life and the lives of those she listened to and cared for; it could never remain abstract, nor lie beyond the reach of questioning – not least her own. It takes courage and generosity to make oneself the mixing bowl in this way. The food that emerges is more than can be found pre-packed and piled high on supermarket shelves; but those involved in its making must learn to be content with active stirring and patient waiting.

The priest as prophet

> 'Before I formed you in the womb I knew you,
> And before you were born I consecrated you;
> I appointed you a prophet to the nations ...
> Now I have put my words in your mouth.
> See, today I appoint you over nations and over kingdoms,
> to pluck up and to pull down,
> to destroy and overthrow,
> to build and to plant.'[28]

Within the major Christian faith communities we lack a distinct order of prophets – or should that be 'disorder' of prophets, given their awkward tendencies as expressed in Old and New Testaments! The principal ministries listed by Paul – prophet among them – were gathered together within the model of priesthood that emerged. Like a prophet, a priest is charged with nourishing people with the word of God. Just as with the prophets, the words they speak are to emerge from a stance of contemplative attentiveness, where the wisdom of Scripture and events of life are held together in dialogue. The open ear, the watchful eye and the attentive spirit are the necessary starting places of any words a true prophet speaks. In company with the prophets, a priest will often feel unworthy or incapable of the task, and have to draw deeply once more on their dependence on God.

Often what a prophet has to say is challenging and goes against the tide of prevailing attitudes and social norms. But this awkwardness is not the priest's own: it flows from the awkwardness of God. God's simplicity confounds the complexity of the myriad ways we find to guard our own interests or live out our fears. The teacher or preacher has to recognize the power they hold. They can use it to reinforce

---

[28] Jeremiah 1.5, 9–10.

their own set of beliefs and impose these on others. They can stand on their own authority and proclaim their own truths. Or they can open themselves to be questioned, challenged, invited and comforted by the living word of God and allow what they share to come from that place.

Sometimes silence can be eloquent. A priest whose homilies I always found worth listening to stood up one Sunday after the Gospel, came to the microphone and said, 'Today, I have nothing to say', and sat down again. That too felt like a word emerging – with authenticity – from the meeting place of God and his human fragility; we have nothing to say if it is not given. He didn't try the same move every week!

A prophet's life reaches beyond religious institutions into nations and kingdoms. While some Old Testament prophets were attached to Temple worship, the figures whose words light up the Scriptures often lived on the margins. The place of John the Baptist was not the synagogue but the wilderness and the river bank. The prophets preferred the practice of justice and mercy to the niceties of correct ritual within worship. The prophetic tradition in the modern world finds expression in the words and actions of lay people as much as priests. But in so far as priesthood also draws inspiration from these people who dared to make themselves available to look, listen and act, then part of the prayerful mission of a priest is to leave the sanctuary behind and wander with God through the places people live and work, buy and sell, debate and legislate. This too is where the word of God is spoken, and waits to be heard. Set aside some time each week to go without agenda to where people are: the shopping centre, the school gates, the community playground, the industrial estate, the residential street and the corners where the homeless find some shelter. Here too are places for *lectio divina*. Look and learn; listen to the people you meet and to the God you meet through them. The word of God is stirring.

Pilgrim traveller

'Were not our hearts burning within us while he was talking to us on the road, while he was opening the scriptures to us?'[29]

We know the story well. Two disciples walk away from Jerusalem and away from their hope. A stranger joins them and encourages them to retell what has taken place for them. Weaving the Scriptures with their experience, the stranger helps them see the work of God afresh. In the moment of recognition he leaves them; but they remember how their hearts burned within as he talked with them along the road.

So much of the experience of those first disciples was associated with movement. The invitation to follow Jesus challenged those who responded to many hard miles along a spiritual, emotional and physical road. I wonder whether this physical movement made changes at the levels of heart, mind and soul more possible. Travel of any kind makes where we customarily live and work less mentally encompassing: there are other worlds out there and different ways of living. We can begin to see beyond the set forms of our current existence; there are other possibilities. For those who went with Jesus, 'follow me' turned out to be more about transformation than destination. From the moment their feet set upon the path, their understanding of who they were and what their lives were for was on the move.

The pattern finds echoes throughout the Bible. Abram, the father of faith, sets out from the security of what he has for a land he does not know. The slaves of Egypt come to a new understanding of their own identity and their liberating God through their wanderings in the desert. Those exiled in Babylon begin a long journey home. The rhythms of journey remind the Jewish people of the foundations of their past, present and future. The Gospels are framed around Jesus' travels up to Jerusalem for the three great feasts of the year. No wonder that the first name associated with the followers of Jesus was 'the Way':[30] a pattern of life *and* an unfinished and continuing journey.

---

[29] Luke 24.32.
[30] Acts 9.2.

Why is movement so central within the biblical narrative? Journeying expresses openness to the invitation of God. God is always 'other', beyond our capacity for comprehension or control. This God is always summoning us beyond our restricted view of who we are and what we are capable of. The danger in settling down is that we domesticate God and limit ourselves. Instead of putting up the traveller's tent we build a house in walls of stone; then we lock inside it an understanding of God we are comfortable with and expectations of ourselves we can manage.

What does this all mean for the Church and for those who serve it as priests? In the face of fast-changing physical landscapes within our neighbourhoods, and the relentless pace of technological innovation, it is unsurprising that many look to the Church for stability. The proposed moving of a pew can be enough to cause a riot. The Church provides the stability of truth amid the strong winds of change. But where does this truth and stability lie? While it is true that the familiarity of times of services, the layout of church buildings, or the particular ways statements of belief or moral guidance are stated can provide reassurance, these are not our place of rest. Our truth and stability abide only within the encounter with God through Christ. For those first disciples travelling along the road, the landscape was always changing; what remained constant was the company of Jesus, Walking with him, received truths were always being refreshed and deepened in meaning. In *Gaudete et exsultate*, Pope Francis warns of the danger of the Church becoming 'a museum piece'. If we 'give excessive importance to certain rules, customs and ways of acting' the Gospel is 'reduced and constricted'.[31] 'God', he affirms, is 'eternal newness' who 'impels us constantly to set out anew, to pass beyond what is familiar, to the fringes and beyond'.[32] The message is all the more powerful coming from one who is at the heart of the weightiest of institutions. Years of history, volumes of legislation, hierarchies of order can stand in the way of responding to the devastating simplicity of Jesus' call: 'Follow me ... leave everything aside':

---

[31] *Gaudete et exsultate* 58.
[32] 135.

True enough we need to open the door of our hearts to Jesus, who stands and knocks (cf. Rev 3:20). Sometimes I wonder, though, if perhaps Jesus is already inside us and knocking on the door to let him escape from our stale self-centredness.[33]

The analogy with a museum is one Pope Francis returns to: perhaps unsurprisingly, given his physical surroundings within the Vatican with its layers of history and custom. Christian life, he insists, involves more than acting as 'a museum of memories'. We are challenged to allow the Holy Spirit to cause us to 'contemplate history in the light of the risen Jesus so that the Church will not stand still, but constantly welcome the Lord's surprises'.[34] Francis is not dismissing the value of tradition. Like a museum the Church has the vital task of conserving and communicating the past: the history of God's working and our story as God's people; the lessons gleaned over time about practices and attitudes that shape us for cooperation with the Spirit; the truths we have received about God, humanity and the created world. But the Church is also the temple of the living God who encounters us afresh in the present moment. We do not look among the dead for one who is living.

If the Church is more than a museum, then priests are more than its curators, carefully ordering and conserving the articles in the collection, and ensuring that those who enter observe proper etiquette. This was a hard lesson for the first disciples. As inheritors of their faith tradition they knew what standards of practice were required of new believers; they were sure about who could and who could not join their number. But then Peter had an awkward dream about eating food that was unclean, and the Holy Spirit came down in force on a Gentile household. As much as they might want to settle down, the God who is 'eternal newness' impelled them to 'set out anew, beyond the familiar' to lands they could not yet know.

Every Sunday priests ask their congregations to stand and proclaim the faith that joins them as a people. Creeds are not ways we define God; God defies definition. Instead they provide a shape for a journey into and from the encounter with God that lies beyond

---

[33] *Gaudete et exsultate* 136.
[34] *Gaudete et exsultate* 139.

the compass of words. Creeds flow from the experience of walking with God and lead us back into walking with God. They are not for standing still.

To be a pilgrim

> Who would true valour see,
> Let him come hither
> One here will constant be
> Come wind, come weather.
> There's no discouragement
> Shall make him once relent
> His first avowed intent
> To be a pilgrim.[35]

Within their own experience, and in ministering to those under their care, priests face a paradox. On the one hand life flows from the stillness of abiding in God, and the truths revealed through that relationship. On the other, life is continual movement in response to a God who is not dead, but alive. We are invited to leave our houses of stone for the adventure of pilgrimage. What will we discover along the way? What will we become?

From where I live it takes me just over half an hour to walk downhill into Canterbury – a centre of pilgrimage since the death of Thomas Becket in 1170. One of the first books to be published in English – *The Canterbury Tales* – tells the story of a group of pilgrims who shared the road from London to Becket's shrine. For many of them the pilgrimage was not only a journey to a sacred place; it was also a holiday, an adventure, and a chance to step out of the demands and constrictions of the normal patterns of their lives. When April comes, Chaucer wrote, the sap rises in human spirits as much as in trees and flowers; people long to tread new paths and see new lands. Perhaps there is in each of us – however well buried – an adventurer who longs to travel new roads. From his very beginnings Jesus was such a traveller. Joseph and Mary took him each year on pilgrimage to Jerusalem for the feast of Passover: a duty of the Law no doubt, but

---

[35] John Bunyan, 1684, *The Pilgrim's Progress*.

also an adventure, and fun. They walked in the company of friends and relatives. They shared food, laughter and stories, old and new; so much so, that on one occasion they even forgot to check their son was with them and had to retrace their steps to Jerusalem. As a grown man, Jesus remained a pilgrim. His first avowed intent was to go where his Father led him, come wind, come weather.

How can priests remain faithful to the pilgrim within their own spirit? How do they wake the adventurer within those they serve? The pressures that lead to inertia can be large. At a collective level we tend to prefer the security of what we know. Change is unsettling. The same may be true for individuals. There is enough to cope with as things are without having to embrace new practices or adopt fresh attitudes. But this is rarely the whole story. At a deeper level we are often disturbed by our restlessness and our dreams. We feel what we lack; we yearn for the unknown 'more'. Ultimately – as Archbishop Helder Camara affirmed – we are not made for standing still:

> Pilgrim: when your ship,
> long moored in harbour, gives you the illusion of being a house;
> when your ship begins to put down roots in the stagnant water by the quay:
> put out to sea!
> Save your boat's journeying soul,
> and your own pilgrim soul,
> cost what it may.[36]

One answer to collective or individual inertia might be to take up the ancient and new practice of pilgrimage. Lest we begin to believe that we have arrived in terms of understanding God, ourselves, or the meaning and purpose of our existence, a physical journey can disturb us out of our torpor and draw us into the adventure of discovering what our lives might become.

There is a resurgence of interest in pilgrimage. The *Camino de Santiago* attracts vast numbers. The motivations for making the journey are as diverse as the people who walk its paths: a search for a new direction in life, the desire to have time to adjust to an unexpected

---

[36] Dom Helder Camara, 1981, *A Thousand Reasons for Living*, London: Darton, Longman & Todd.

and life-changing event, a physical challenge, or a different holiday experience. For many of those who walk, the outcomes of the journey are unanticipated; life will never be quite the same. The daily setting out into the unknown, dependence on the kindness of strangers, and the stripping away of so much that in 'ordinary life' was judged essential, shakes up their view of who they are, what their lives are for, and – for some at least – who God is.

Not everyone has the leisure or the resources to walk the *Camino*. But the practice of pilgrimage can take root in smaller ways. What if – as local churches – we made one Sunday Eucharist a year a pilgrim journey? The journey doesn't have to be of life-threatening dimensions. We can choose as destination a place of commonly recognized spiritual significance – for example, another local church, or a nearby historical site associated with prayer. It can be a day, morning or afternoon's journey rather than one of several weeks. At the end of this chapter are some practical considerations for planning such a pilgrimage and weaving within it a rhythm of reflection and prayer. I am not pretending that such a journey will have the same life-changing effects as walking the *Camino* or the Pilgrims Way to Canterbury. But even small movements create momentum. The feet get used to walking. A different order of conversation takes place when we walk side by side along a shared road. We feel the fresh air, not just of the outdoors but of the Spirit of God. If we enjoy the experience we might look for more opportunities or more testing journeys. I am often struck by how few men dare to go to anything that smacks of prayer, spiritual practice or sharing. But it might well be that men will walk and find themselves at home doing just those things in the course of a pilgrim journey. Sometimes we recognize that a local church could do with the loosening up that a shared walk invites. We begin to realize that being together doesn't always have to be solemn; it might sometimes be fun. Holidays can be holy days.

At a more personal level there may be times when a priest needs a similar pilgrim journey made alone or with trusted friends. It's possible to become hemmed in by tasks and expectations. The inner spirit runs dry. Rather than become locked into keeping going even when our 'going' has gone, it can help to set out afresh along a physical road. We need no agenda; there is nothing to achieve save putting one step in front of another. Walking the road we begin to sense the presence of a stranger who seems to understand our journey; we experience a different form of heartburn.

Where do I go? The need for discernment

The course of a journey is shaped by its chosen destination. Some years ago I walked the Offa's Dyke Path, a long-distance trail following the ancient boundary between England and Wales. I chose to travel south to north, beginning near Chepstow and ending at Prestatyn. The question that I carried with me through the journey was a practical one: 'Where do I go?' This was easy enough to resolve in those stretches where the signposts were clear or when I could see ahead of me the next village I was making for. At other times there seemed no obvious answer. The signposts had a habit of leading me into deep woods, where numerous competing paths branched out in different directions, and then deserting me. On one high hilltop I became disorientated in a dank fog. My feet stumbled on rocks and slipped in mud. I was aware there were steep drops around me. The 'path' I thought I was following had long since disappeared. I got the map from my rucksack to make out roughly where I was. The name of the place was 'World's End'. Thanks for that information! Later, when asked by friends for the mileage of the Offa's Dyke Path, the honest answer I gave was, 'It depends on how many times you get lost.'

'Where do I go?' is the defining question of any journey made into unknown ground. The beginning of the answer lies in remembering where it is we want to get to. This is the foundation of discernment. In the process of deciding what path to follow we keep in mind where it is we are travelling to. In the larger picture of Christian discipleship there are many competing formulations of the end and means of our journey, but within the limits of words, here seem to be some common threads:

- We are travelling deeper into relationship with God, in response to the invitation of the Spirit.
- In allowing ourselves to be drawn into greater intimacy with God we open ourselves to a process of transformation. It is

God who brings about this transformation, through our chosen cooperation.

- This process of transformation sets us free to live the truth of who we are. This involves both the shedding of attitudes and patterns of behaviour that diminish us, and the emergence and growth of all that God has created us to be.
- We grow with and through one another. Our relationships with other people and the created world are the proving ground of our movement into the fullness of our being.
- The fullness of our being – expressed individually and within our relationships – images God in the generosity of our giving and receiving. Our lives become creative and fruitful through our openness to the creative and fruitful Spirit of God.

Here then is the orientation of our travel; we move as individuals and in mutual dependence with others. Beyond personal fulfilment this journey involves us in working with God to make all creation new. Not a step can be made without the grace of God. Every footfall rests on cooperation with the Spirit.

When there are so many pulls on our energies and desires from media in all its forms, social and political movements, our own fears and needs, and a myriad of external expectations, it helps to keep in mind the orientation of our travel. In this choice before me, am I moving with the direction of the Spirit or against it? For priests the challenge of discernment has more than one layer. They have to make choices that impact on the future of their church. The nature of their guidance and support will influence the direction of travel of the lives of those they care for. Before all, they must listen to the pushes and pulls of their own desires: 'Where is the Spirit at work in my life? What movement is invited of me at this time? What am I to do? Where do I go?' Without a regular practice of discernment it will be difficult to find our way out of the forest or beyond 'World's End'.

What's in a day? The *examen*

The *examen* is a simple way of remembering the day with God. Many priests practise some form of it; night prayer of the daily Office includes a space for it. More than one priest I have spoken to has shared how this one way of prayer, beyond all others, provides an anchor that holds them in relationship with God and enables them to maintain their equilibrium. The *examen* is often associated with becoming aware of our faults and then seeking forgiveness and conversion of life. This is one dimension of the practice. We grow in self-awareness by reviewing our inward and outward responses to what happened in our day and the people we encountered. However, the *examen* does not only focus on looking at ourselves: its purpose is also to develop our awareness of the presence of God and the daily invitations of the Spirit. This is the perspective from which we view our own behaviour. The *examen* is also a means of developing our capacity for discernment; it is a prayer for those who are travelling and seeking direction – a prayer of orientation and reorientation. I think of those moments when on a physical journey I stop to check whether I am still on the right path. I review the choices I made that brought me to this place: I question how mindful I was of where the true path lay: did I miss a hidden turning, or too quickly assume that because this was a broad track it must be the right one? I unfold the map once more and consider where I go from here.

Here is one framework for making a daily *examen*:

I remember I am in God's presence

Throughout this prayer it will be God who guides me, so I open myself to God's presence with me and love for me. It may help to picture myself in a Gospel scene as I do so. Perhaps I am walking in Jesus' company along the road to Emmaus and we are reviewing my experience of the day together. Or perhaps I am there with Peter by the lakeside and we are talking heart to heart about what has taken place.

I remember with gratitude the gifts of the day

I ask God to help me recall with gratitude the gifts of the day, however small and easily passed by. As I remember and give thanks, I am opening myself to the goodness of God, the wonders of creation and the blessings brought by all that has given joy to my spirit.

I review my experience of the day

I replay my day, letting God prompt my memory. I ask God's help in recognizing significant moments, and times when my feelings or thoughts were particularly stirred.

I ask for understanding

Do I sense some invitation of the Spirit in what took place today? Perhaps I was blind to it then but I see it now. I ask for insight into my own responses. How far was I cooperating with the Spirit? What else was driving my reactions?

I let go to God my need of healing and wholeness

I own my need of God in those areas where I struggled today. I trust myself to God's continuing love and labour for me.

I trust myself to God for tomorrow

In the light of my reflection I give to God my desire to amend my thoughts, attitudes and responses in the day to come. I acknowledge my dependence on God's grace. I rest any fears or burdens in God's care.

Practised consistently the *examen* helps us be more aware of the guidance of the Spirit amid the muddle of our experience. At the unanticipated time the stranger breaks bread and our eyes open to what is real and true. We come to recognize that we never travel alone.

Spiritual direction

Most priests will have been encouraged (or told) to get a spiritual director during their discernment process or training. While many priests in ministry continue to see a spiritual director on a regular basis, a significant number now have no one they can relate to in this way. The reasons are varied:

- One or other side in the relationship moves away.
- The first experience of spiritual direction is not a positive one.
- There is difficulty in finding someone who enables sufficient depth of engagement.

- Accidental drifting apart takes place when the pressures of ministry are great.
- Priests are often not very good at looking after their own interests.
- There was a mismatch of expectations as to the purpose of spiritual direction that created dissatisfaction or puzzlement as to what it was all about anyway.

All the above are understandable reasons why a priest has no one to turn to who can support them on their journey with God. Yet, I believe, we do all need someone. In what follows I will briefly outline my understanding of what lies at the heart of spiritual direction, and then share why I think it is vital for priests.

Spiritual direction centres on attentiveness to the Spirit. As Jesus told Nicodemus, the Spirit is like the wind: we hear its sound but we do not know where it comes from or where it goes.[37] Each individual spiritual journey is unique. When I accompany another as a spiritual director I have to continually let go any agendas I might have about what this person should be or do. The future is a mystery to me as it is to the person I am listening to. My role is not to tell people what to do but to help them engage with God openly and generously. The primary relationship is always between God and the person. A spiritual director seeks to serve that relationship by supporting those they accompany in reviewing their experience with God. Where is the invitation of the Spirit amid all that this person has experienced, heard, seen, sensed or understood? In what way might they respond to this invitation?

Though there is no precise map for a person's life, there is a general sense of orientation. As disciples we are travelling deeper into God, and God is moving more actively into our lives, through faith, hope and love. Through cooperation with the Spirit, and engagement with others, we are moving more fully into the truth of our individual being. Through choosing to abide in God our lives become fruitful: we come to share the best of ourselves in a way that is life-giving for others. Regular conversation with a spiritual director can keep us in the flow of that orientation; we all lose track now and then of the direction we want to travel. There is a place for the director's

---

[37] John 3.8.

experience in helping those they accompany stay in that flow: they can help us explore ways of prayer that work with the realities of our life and personality; through careful listening they help us sift through our experience and notice where we have been stirred in some way; when we are down on ourselves they can mirror back to us the loving acceptance of God.

Why does receiving quality spiritual direction matter for priests? Not because they are *more important* to God than anyone else but because they are *equally important*. When we have care of others we easily forget to care for ourselves. Priests listen to people – and they need to be listened to. Priests encourage others to seek God – and they need this encouragement themselves. When I have the privilege of accompanying a priest as a spiritual director I try to look at them not just as a servant to their parish but as a person who has physical, emotional, social and spiritual needs, since – I believe – God sees them this way too. God wants you to 'be' with all the being that is in you. Though your service may earth you in one place, you remain a pilgrim, and adventure lies ahead of you. You have responsibility for many, but you are never lost in the crowd, for God never ceases to see you and labour for you. Allow God to take you seriously.

To be a pilgrim: putting it into practice

What follows are some starting points for considering whether a physical pilgrimage might be helpful for you or for your church, together with some practical suggestions for planning a pilgrimage and giving it a sense of sacred journey.

Why make a pilgrimage?

- To express the desire for a deeper commitment to God.
- To seek discernment: what does it mean for me at this point in my life to follow Christ?
- To have space to come to terms with a life-changing event.
- To re-view one's life and priorities in the light of relationship with God.
- As a means of repentance: the journey expresses the desire to turn away from an old way of life that is deadening and destructive and to follow a new path that is creative and life-giving.

- To escape convenient comforts that limit our capacity for life and love.
- In simple terms – because the journey and/or the destination draws me – and who knows what might happen along the way?
- To journey with others in friendship, mutual support, remaining open to learn and grow from new experiences.

What is it about 'pilgrimage' that makes it such a powerful experience?

- It is intentional: the one choice is to make the journey. Everything we experience moment by moment and day by day flows from this.
- In this sense pilgrimage mirrors Christian discipleship: we choose to follow Christ along the way, through the stuff of life.
- One person described it as 'a holiday from freedom'. Paradoxically the choice we make and renew each day to walk the path liberates us from being slave to every whim and passing desire.
- Journeying disturbs us out of set patterns and enables us to review our life and priorities.
- Events happen along the way that we do not anticipate; some we welcome, others we find challenging. We are brought into a raw, honest place where we become able to see ourselves and to recognize our dependence on God.
- We learn from fellow travellers and from strangers we meet along the way.
- We regain a spirit of adventure.
- We come to a place that has spiritual significance for us.
- Though we might start with a fixed idea about what the pilgrimage will bring, the experience is likely to surprise us: the outcome will not be as we imagined.

A pilgrimage for a church or group

Though we walk an individual path of Christian discipleship through our particular life circumstances, we also travel with one another. We are people of the Way and a shared pilgrimage expresses our common dedication to seeking the kingdom of God here on earth, as in heaven. Travelling companions support one another and share their provisions. A journey made together can reinforce this sense of common identity and purpose. Friendships are made, life stories are shared and barriers are broken down. A pilgrimage made together, where we draw on the friendship and practical support of others to sustain us, expresses how all of life has this same pattern. There is no individual salvation that does not take account of love of neighbour.

A pilgrimage also reminds us as Church that we have not yet arrived. We are always, as a community, open to move on in response to the leading of the Spirit. Changes will happen around us and we are challenged to respond to them. We are followers of the risen Jesus who is still on the move, actively seeking to teach, heal and reconcile.

Planning your pilgrimage

Who is it for?
Your individual response to God … a group that has a common task or purpose … members of your church … open to all including the family and friends of church members and local people who feel drawn by the challenge?

What are the limits of time, mobility and cost?
Not everyone will be able to afford a pilgrimage to the Holy Land or be able to take a week off to walk to Canterbury. These are not reasons in themselves not to do these things but it's important to recognize the challenges. If you only have a day or an afternoon, it is still possible to do something worthwhile and without financial cost.

Where will you go?
This will in part be governed by who the pilgrimage is for and practical considerations of time and cost, but also thoughts of what place has spiritual significance for you. The nature of the route will also be a consideration.

What will your route be?
Safety is one consideration. It will neither be wise nor pleasant to walk miles along the verge of a busy dual carriageway! Is there a

route by footpath? If people have different levels of mobility is the path suitable? If you are planning a group pilgrimage it's helpful to walk the route in advance to identify what the problems might be and where you might have to seek alternatives. This will also be helpful in giving you a more realistic view of how long the journey will take. You'll also want to make the path interesting, taking in different types of scenery (whether urban or rural), local landmarks, viewpoints and stopping points.

What provisions will you need to take?

This will depend in part on how long your trip will be. Enough food and drink, a good map, suitable clothing and footwear will be important, but without weighing you down impossibly. If planning a trip for a group it might be helpful to provide a guidance sheet on what to take / not take.

Where will you stop / stay?

If staying overnight then planning accommodation will be important. Even if people bring food to eat or share, you might still want to build in the opportunity to visit a pub or café for refreshment and celebration.

How will you make your pilgrimage a spiritual experience?

A pilgrimage is about a destination and a journey. A physical place is travelled to, but each person will have a sense of personal quest: a something they are looking for, a path they are seeking to follow in their life. Then there are the ups and downs of the journey itself: feeling tired or lost; questioning why I set out; gazing in wonder at a beautiful skyline; being overcome with a sense of personal achievement about having climbed that hill or walked that far. It is helpful to create the frameworks where people can reflect and share about their pilgrimage experiences and the ways these resonate with movements in their lives.

The backdrop lies within so many biblical stories: Abraham, Jacob, Moses' journey into the wilderness, the Exodus, the Exile and return, the pilgrim songs within the psalms, the invitation of Jesus to 'Follow me', the road to Jerusalem, the Emmaus Road, the early Church named as 'the Way' ... and so on. Some of these passages could be recounted in the course of the journey

In a real sense, the space given to travelling, the miles walked alone or in the company of others, and the desire people hold in their hearts will give depth and meaning to the experience without doing anything more. Having said this, here are some other ways of enriching the experience:

A liturgy of blessing for those beginning the pilgrimage
This might include some of the following:

- One of the pilgrimage psalms (120–134).
- Genesis 28.20–33, Jacob's vow.
- A pilgrim hymn.
- Each person taking two stones: one symbolizing their intent in making this journey and one for a burden or concern they currently carry and wish to place with God.

On a longer journey
Providing a rhythm of simple prayers and readings over the days of the pilgrimage, for example morning, evening or night prayer of the Daily Office.

A quiet, reflective personal time of walking within each day
'For the first half hour we will stay in a quiet place as we walk, to make space to be present to God.'

An 'Emmaus walk' at some point in the journey
Walking and sharing with one other person, perhaps chosen at random, about the personal journey that this outward journey expresses.

A point in the journey when people release their burdens and concerns
Letting go or throwing away the stones they have carried. An alternative might be to make a small cairn with the stones, or to lay them out in the shape of a cross.

An individual or group examen within the day, where people can simply and prayerfully remember their day's journey with God and what it has meant for them

- What good things did I see or experience today that I can thank God for?
- How did God speak to me today in what I saw, felt or heard?
- What do I want to let go to God: an anxiety, my wrongdoing, or my need of healing?

An arrival liturgy – with opportunity to share what the experience has meant in personal terms

This might include some of the following:

- One of the pilgrimage psalms.
- A pilgrim hymn.
- Space for each person to speak in turn about the personal significance of their journey.
- A prayer of blessing for the next steps in our journey with God.

5

Rain for Roots:
The Priest as Minister

Servant

'You know that among the Gentiles those whom they recognize as their rulers lord it over them, and their great ones are tyrants over them. But it is not so among you; but whoever wishes to become great among you must be your servant, and whoever wishes to be first among you must be the slave of all. For the Son of Man came not to be served but to serve, and to give his life as a ransom for many.'[1]

We tend to be wary of owning the power that we have – unsurprisingly perhaps, since examples of the destructive use of power abound. Those who like to 'lord it over' others often end up oppressing or exploiting them. But we do have power, and rather than deny its existence we have to look at it, own it and decide how we will use it. As a curate I felt more aware of the power I lacked: living in another's house, subject to being moved at short notice at the will of the bishop, and under the authority of parish priests whose views on matters often differed from my own. But for all this the power at my disposal was considerable. As an ordained minister I was presumed to be an authority on the Bible and Church teaching. At the lectern I had the choice as to what to say in response to the readings of the day. Aware of my position, or through sight of my uniform, people shared personal difficulties with me even though I lacked their length of years or life experience. With some of my time at least, I could choose what work I focused on and

---

[1] Mark 10.42–45.

who I gave space to. When someone called at the presbytery door I could welcome them in or send them away.

Power in itself is neither good nor bad. What matters is how we use it. Do you ever pause to think what power you wield when you drive a car? Potentially every time you turn on the ignition you start into life a dangerous weapon capable of untold destruction. That's not the intended purpose of the vehicle, but the car will only be safe if the driver chooses to honour other people on the road and actively manages their desire to get to the destination in the shortest possible time. Our present times bear witness to what happens when those in authority fail to recognize how their use of power impacts upon the lives of the most vulnerable, or use their authority to serve their own ends. Jesus gave his disciples authority and showed them by his own life how to use it:

- *for* the wellbeing of others
- *against* all that diminishes and oppresses
- *for* movement towards community
- *to* create and build up
- *for* the washing of tired feet.

God chooses to be the servant of all creation – the continuing source of its being and becoming. Humility is God's chosen way.

Every priest has to decide – moment by moment – how they will use the power given to them. The choice is one of stance: what or who do I serve? Whose cause do I labour for? Will I use authority to create or destroy, to build up or knock down? The questions faced by Jesus in the wilderness continued to echo throughout his ministry: Will I use my power to meet my own needs, or trust that those needs will be cared for if I rest my life in God? Will I make people bow down to me, or will I give what I have in their service? Will I dazzle them into adoring compliance or, as a companion, break bread with them? Aware of the seductive allure of using power for personal advantage, Jesus faced his disciples with the surprise of his own stance: 'the Son of Man came not to be served but to serve'.

Jesus invited his disciples to engage with a paradox: to have authority, and know you have it, so that you can use it to serve other people's needs and, where possible, give it away. Those who came from Jesus' home town wondered at the force of his teaching. The crowds who followed him marvelled at the way he found means to feed the hungry and heal the sick. When challenged whether he had the right to forgive sins and overturn the bonds of injustice, Jesus did not hesitate to confront his accusers and demonstrate the legitimacy of his authority. Here was a powerful man. You have to know your power to use it. And yet Jesus resolutely refrained from forcing another to follow him or conform to his will. He chose instead to honour their choices. His way was to come alongside and to build people up. Sometimes he challenged them; always, he invited them to choose where life lay. But he refused to use his power to control or manipulate their responses. The power of God is expressed in creativity. Domination narrows the life of the other; creation continually enlarges it. The one who dominates fears freedom and seeks to suppress it. The one who creates delights in the independent being of the other. Jesus came to bring life in its abundance; the one who dominates 'steals, kills and destroys'.[2]

God is not – as we sometimes imagine – made in our image; instead we are to be remade in God's image. We betray our preferences when we address God as 'almighty'; we warm to the idea that we too – in God's likeness – might gain such a position. But the almighty God of our dreams casts all away. The all-humble God chooses the stable, the carpenter's bench, the company of tax collectors and sinners, and the cross as fitting places to be at home. God stoops low to serve us, and in this movement the height and breadth of the creative power of love is revealed. For disciples then and now, for those in authority, and for priests, the challenges are real:

- How can we own and use the power we have as a gift and a needed resource, rather than bury it in the ground out of fear?
- How are we to use the authority we have creatively, for life, and for the wellbeing of those whose lives we touch?
- How will we renounce the use of power as a means of shoring up our own empires through the domination and exploitation of others?

---

[2] John 10.10.

Practising humility

> 'Come to me, all you that are weary and are carrying heavy burdens, and I will give you rest. Take my yoke upon you, and learn from me; for I am gentle and humble in heart, and you will find rest for your souls. For my yoke is easy, and my burden is light.'[3]

We met this passage before in the context of Jesus' invitation to be with him. Here I want to draw on these pivotal words to explore what the practice of humility looks like. The two phrases that frame 'learn from me' are 'take my yoke upon you' and 'for I am gentle and humble in heart'. The yoke that gives rest and eases burdens is humility of heart. This yoke is not imposed, but taken up freely and placed over consenting shoulders. Humility of heart is Jesus' yoke; he invites us to make it ours too. 'Heart' suggests more than something put on for show: this choice works from the inside out – from the chosen orientation of the will to outward actions. What is humility of heart? If it expresses Jesus' chosen stance to life then there is nothing here about fearful subservience or cringing self-deprecation. The humble Jesus is also the authoritative Jesus who stands up against injustice and for the dignity of each human person. Humility concerns not getting in the way, and avoiding tripping up over our oversized egos. The humble person is self-aware but not self-obsessed. Rowan Williams put it this way:

> To be the means of reconciliation for another within the Body of Christ, you must be consciously yourself, knowing a bit about what has made you who you are, what your typical problems and brick walls are, what your gifts are.[4]

The ability to make creative use of personal gifts while maintaining an active wariness of personal vulnerability is not easy to find or keep. In the wilderness Jesus chooses the yoke of resting in relationship with the Father as the source of his self-knowledge and as guardian of his self-expression. 'Learn from me,' he urges. You will only learn

---

[3] Matthew 11.28–30.
[4] Rowan Williams, 2004, *Silence and Honeycakes: The wisdom of the desert*, Oxford: Lion Books.

who you are and become the more you can be if you are rooted and grounded in the goodness of God. Relationship with God is our place of rest. Here we discover a truth that sets us free from fruitless anxiety about our status, our worth, or our degree of personal perfection. Here our imperfections are held with love; we can begin to face them without fear – and with God's help – grow from them. We can also own our gifts and use them without reticence or embarrassment; after all, they are God's work in us, and meant for sharing.

The opportunities to grow in humility come in droves within the ordinary course of daily life. We have no need of barefoot walks up stony paths, hair shirts or self-flagellation. Take yesterday when I went to Tesco in a rush to buy one thing. Queues stretched behind the 'express checkouts'. Then I saw my opportunity: an empty checkout with two members of staff talking with each other; no one else seemed to have noticed the space. I unloaded my one item. My triumph lasted a brief moment: 'This checkout is closed,' one of the women at the counter said cheerfully. 'But there's nothing to say it's closed,' I objected, inwardly outraged. She smiled gently and informed me that I had put my one item down on the staff side rather than the customer side; had I approached it the right way I would have seen the sign. Without grace, I joined another queue. She was absolutely right: I had made a mistake. She was also courteous and understanding in her response. So why was I worked up? As I walked from the shop I began to make enquiry of my troubled spirit, and my thoughts led me to the meeting I was hurrying towards. I had never found the person I was going to see easy; through no fault of his own he woke memories of other people who had once made my life difficult. I was going into this meeting with my barbed wire to the fore, ready for conflict. I passed the door of an open church, and though time was now pressing, I went in and sat down.

I needed to let all this out – all 'me' out – before God. I had no remedy for my tensed-up self other than this. I didn't want what belonged to the past to impact on the present. I needed God's help for this. I could look on my prickly self without condemnation, since God looked on me with compassion. As I stayed there under the gaze of God, a freer space began to develop within. I could uncurl my clenched fists and approach the meeting to come with openness, rather than defensiveness.

The practice of humility goes something like this. We open up how we are before God, asking God to help us understand where the fears and needs that drive us stem from. The picture may not be pretty – to us at least. But rather than run from it, in facing what we feel we also face God. There we can take responsibility for what belongs to us rather than pile up our fault-finding on those inconvenient and disagreeable others. Rather than react, we can choose to act. Instead of drowning in self-blame we find a resting place in God's compassionate gaze on us in our incompleteness. There we see reflected God's unwavering hope for us – a hope we can actively cooperate with day by day as we move further into the truth of who we are.

The *examen* and humility

I have described how the practice of a daily *examen* enables us to be more aware of God's leading and guiding within the busy movement of daily life. The *examen* can also help us to go on aligning our lives with our humble God. As I reflect on the day with God I notice my reactions to what took place. I review my responses: my feelings and the actions that followed from them. I consider what was moving me: was it love or fear, a concern for my own status or the heartfelt desire to build another up? How did I choose to use the power given to me? The purpose of this examination is not to drown in self-blame but to open ourselves to the mercy of God. I am in the presence of one who welcomes me in my muddle of motivation. I can lay bare my inmost being without fear of rejection. I remember the words of a man who had come to discover God's acceptance of him at a new depth: 'There is nothing of which I am ashamed that Jesus does not love.' Rather than turning us away Jesus puts on the garb of a servant and washes our feet. With Peter, I might want to put up a fight here, but Jesus is insistent: this is how it must be. Accepting – however uneasily – such love, our own capacity for compassion begins to grow. As the letter to the Hebrews reminds us, in recognizing how God meets our weakness we can begin to allow the power of God's merciful love to flow from us to those who are also sometimes difficult, self-centred and all over the place:

> Every high priest chosen from among mortals is put in charge of things pertaining to God on their behalf, to offer gifts and sacrifices for sins. He is able to deal gently with the ignorant and wayward, since he himself is subject to weakness; and because of this he must offer sacrifice for his own sins as well as for those of the people.[5]

The practice of the *examen* also helps us check our stance towards life and ministry. 'Learn from me,' Jesus says, 'for I am gentle and humble in heart.' Humility doesn't come easily. We will probably have to let go again and again of being in the right, having the last word, claiming the glory, or holding on to control. We will see afresh how our fears and insecurities drive us. Once more, the *examen* will invite us into a place of rest, where all our worth, security and fulfilment lie in grounding our lives in God.

If I do not have love

> If I speak in the tongues of mortals and of angels, but do not have love, I am a noisy gong or a clanging cymbal. And if I have prophetic powers, and understand all mysteries and all knowledge, and if I have all faith, so as to remove mountains, but do not have love, I am nothing.[6]

Paul's words on love are often chosen for a wedding, but they are equally appropriate for an ordination service. For priesthood without love is empty of purpose and empty of God. My own sense is that Paul was speaking not only to the Corinthians but to himself. By the time he travelled the Damascus Road Paul was already a preacher, an effective organizer, and a person of influence capable of moving others into action. What changed when Christ broke into his life was not so much the nature of Paul's work, or the gifts he exercised within it, but what moved and shaped his activity. Love – undeserved and poured out in abundance – had healed and freed him. Outside of

---

[5] Hebrews 5.1–3.
[6] 1 Corinthians 13.1–2.

being loved he was no one; without expressing love he could create no-thing. Only love gives being. I feel Paul's fears for himself even as I write these words. How possible it is to weave fine sentences that neither come from God, nor lead to God. How easy it would be for Paul, caught up as he was with so many different projects, to become a clanging cymbal or noisy gong. He knew the danger. He had lived that life. What are priests about if not love? What are sermons, services, mission initiatives or community projects about without love as their motive force?

This is why humility matters: because it leads us back to love as the one and only source of effective ministry. This is why we open ourselves in prayer even when our prayer seems poor and faltering. We need God. We need loving. An unformed and chaotic world awaits the Spirit of creative love to move over its dark waters. We want to be part of that movement: to be a channel for the only voice capable of calling forth, naming and blessing new life in all its wondrous variety. There are already more than enough gongs and cymbals. Love, as Paul describes it, has the physical form of the servant God who comes with power to create, rather than dominate.

Open yourself to the humility of God

> Love is patient; love is kind; love is not envious or boastful or arrogant or rude. It does not insist on its own way; it is not irritable or resentful; it does not rejoice in wrongdoing, but rejoices in the truth. It bears all things, believes all things, hopes all things, endures all things. Love never ends.[7]

When we gaze at a nativity crib or rest our attention on the cross, we behold the humility of God. These physical symbols of our faith invite our sustained attention. We are stripped of our assumptions about how power expresses itself. We are brought afresh before the surprise of God. Paul's writing about the nature of love can work in the same way. We tend to read it as a checklist for all that we aspire to but fall short of. But first and foremost Paul is writing about the nature of God's self expression. Such creativity of life will also begin

---

[7] 1 Corinthians 13.4–7.

to flow through us in so far as we open ourselves to the Spirit. The first and necessary step, however, in receiving these words about love is to contemplate what they tell us about God.

To help with this, read through the passage slowly. Every time you read the word 'love' in the passage above, put 'God' in its place. Pause to let the words soak in. Then read them once more. Now 'look' at this God, and let this God look at you; rest under this gaze. Let slip away anything that does not belong in your previous understanding of who God is and how God is. As you contemplate this love in whose image you are made, you see your own reflection as in a mirror, and the Spirit continues to transform you into the object of your gaze.[8]

Singing the mysteries

> Now we do not give so much attention to the mysteries as to disregard the melody, for these are songs, and prefer to be sung rather than debated. And I doubt whether they can be analysed more clearly than when they are sung.[9]

Those who are humble are more comfortable with mystery than those who attempt to lord it over life and wrestle the unknowable into manageable form. There are limits to what we can know and what we are able to control. We cannot always make things right, or press down what takes place into our preformed containers. Priests celebrate the mysteries of Christ's birth, death and resurrection; they are servants of the Spirit who blows where she wills. Truth is larger than our current understanding and often more surprising.

Rather than being lords of the feast, priests are the waiters. The job title is descriptive: the waiter waits attentively knowing there will be work they need to do, understanding the importance of remaining attentive to another's leading. They know that their contribution is important and that sometimes they must take the initiative to ensure the guests do not go hungry. But the food and the feast is not theirs. Jesus himself took the place of a waiter, seeking to understand and serve

---

[8] 2 Corinthians 3.18.
[9] Gilbert of Hoyland, a twelfth-century Cistercian monk, quoted in Esther de Waal, 1998, *The Way of Simplicity: The Cistercian Tradition*, Traditions of Christian Spirituality Series, London: Darton, Longman & Todd, p. 60.

his Father's desire. This led him into situations that were not wholly in his hands and towards outcomes hidden from his understanding. Following in his way we too become servants of mysteries beyond our reach. We take hold of what is given us to see and do, and we let go of our need to always know what the answer is or wholly determine how the enterprise will turn out. There is a place for debate and analysis and a place for singing a song that is not of our making.

Taking hold and letting go is the way of the servant. Perhaps I am listening to someone sharing their story and looking for its meaning. I take hold of my responsibility to make room for this person, to listen with attention, to help them explore their experience and bring it to their own listening place before God. I let go of providing the answer or telling them what to do. If I see a need in my community, I take hold of my commitment to act and not sit idly by, and I let go of believing that the only valid perspective on what needs to be done is mine.

Taking hold and letting go can also become the shape of prayer:

I take hold of my concern for this person or this situation.
I let go to God whatever part I might play, or not play, in addressing this concern.

I take hold of my ideas and my plans.
I let my ideas and plans go into the stream of God's working.

I take hold of my desire to have an answer now.
I let go to God in trust and I consent to waiting.

I take hold of my desire to have things go my way.
I let go to God my need to control what will be.

I take hold of myself with all the insecurities that sometimes drive me.
I let this self go to God, who is healing what is fearful in me.

You will probably find that on another day you will need to let go in this or that area all over again. Letting go is rarely completed in one single movement, but gradually we learn to join in the singing of mystery.

> On the third day there was a wedding in Cana of Galilee, and the mother of Jesus was there. Jesus and his disciples had also been invited to the wedding. When the wine gave out, the mother of Jesus said to him, 'They have no wine' ... Now standing there were six stone water-jars for the Jewish rites of purification, each holding twenty or thirty gallons. Jesus said to them, 'Fill the jars with water' ... When the steward tasted the water that had become wine ... the steward called the bridegroom and said to him, 'Everyone serves the good wine first, and then the inferior wine after the guests have become drunk. But you have kept the good wine until now.'[10]

It was a good party. The food was generous, the songs boisterous and the laughter loud. The wine flowed freely until it flowed no more. The day was saved by the intervention of a guest. How could anyone make sense of how some 150 gallons of water had become the best of wines? It was a very good party!

John names this event the first of Jesus' signs and the revelation of his glory. Water for purification became wine of the Spirit. New life pours out abundantly on this other 'third day'. The union celebrated is not only the wedding of a woman and a man but the bond of belonging between humankind and God. The sharing of the feast expresses the generous giving and receiving of the life of God in which all now partake. Throughout the Gospels Jesus celebrates our belonging to one another through our belonging to God. He sits and eats with tax collectors and sinners, spreads out a table in the wilderness for a hungry crowd and tells the story of a son gone missing who returns home to fatted calf, sandals and a ring. A Passover feast anticipates the sacrificial offering of his own life, given to set an oppressed people free. The risen Lord makes himself known in the breaking of the bread, and heals one who is broken with breakfast on a beach.

No wonder then that the eucharistic feast is central to the life of the Church and the ministry of a priest. Communion is the shape of God's activity: life in its fullness expressed in giving and receiving.

---

[10] John 2.1–10.

Communion is also the life we are shaped for, for it is together, in the pattern of our relationships, that humanity grows into its true identity as an image of the Triune God.

One of the privileges of priests is sharing so intimately in the words and actions of the eucharistic feast. As if to imprint it on their minds priests speak Christ's words afresh: 'This is me. I am for you.' They take bread and wine, give thanks for it and share it with all. This is the pattern of our lives. We freely and gratefully offer who we are; we share out the gift. This is God's way; this is the human way. There is no other path to life. For the one who presides at the Eucharist the movement of the body expresses the journey of the human spirit. The open hands of prayer carry the giving of the mind and will. A priest is a minister of communion. I mean this in its fullest sense: they minister belonging to God and through God our belonging to one another. This is a beautiful gift and a rare privilege.

And yet there are also difficulties for priests in being this focal point within the liturgy. As celebrants they stand in the place of the giver; but communion is also about receiving. Though they take the bread and drink from the cup, no other person places these in their hands. They do not join the queue to stand at the edge of the sanctuary or to kneel at the rail. A priest stands in the place of Christ; but the opportunities are few to receive Christ present for them through the giving of another human being. It is how things are, and the gifts of the role outweigh any loss. And yet something *is* lost by rarely being in the physical place of a receiver, for a priest is a *participant* in this communion as well as its minister; their liturgical role makes this truth more difficult to experience. The architecture of our church buildings tends to tell the same story. For the most part, priests are in the sanctuary, separated from the body of people of whom they are a part.

I am not suggesting we need to reorder all our church buildings or change the structure of the eucharistic liturgy. Rather, I am underlining what might be the underside of the priest's role within worship. Along with entering fully into the prayer of Jesus' self-giving, priests may need to take extra steps to remember and to experience that they are also receivers, as much in need of nurture and belonging as anyone else.

Sitting and eating

George Herbert was an Anglican priest and poet. Priesthood came towards the end of his short life and marked the years when he was most happy and fulfilled. Originally destined for a life at court, priestly ministry drew out his pastoral heart. With his wife their house became a home where many felt welcomed. He found joy in the common celebration of the prayer of the Church within the parish or at nearby Salisbury Cathedral. His love for the Bible and the Eucharist flows through many of his poems. For all this, his relationship with God was not always an easy one, and his struggles to understand the ways of God and to live with his own shortcomings are also reflected in his verse. 'Love bade me welcome' reflects how difficult it can be as a person and as a priest to receive all that another has to give us:

> Love bade me welcome; yet my soul drew back,
>   Guilty of dust and sin.
> But quick-eyed Love, observing me grow slack
>   From my first entrance in,
> Drew nearer to me, sweetly questioning
>   If I lack'd anything.
>
>   'A guest,' I answer'd, 'worthy to be here:'
>   Love said, 'You shall be he.'
> 'I, the unkind, ungrateful? Ah, my dear,
>   I cannot look on Thee.'
> Love took my hand and smiling did reply,
>   'Who made the eyes but I?'
>
>   'Truth, Lord; but I have marr'd them: let my shame
>   Go where it doth deserve.'
> 'And know you not,' says Love, 'Who bore the blame?'
>   'My dear, then I will serve.'
> 'You must sit down,' says Love, 'and taste my meat.'
>   So I did sit and eat.[11]

The 'to and fro' between Love's persistence and the guest's reluctance echoes through the poem. Though Love sees the guest's unease and

---

[11] 'Love (111)', in C. A. Patrides (ed.), 1974, *The English Poems of George Herbert*, London: J. M. Dent & Sons Ltd.

hears all his objections, Love goes on drawing closer. The welcome knows no bounds. Then the guest makes a last-ditch defence: 'then I will serve'. It is easier that way: to follow the familiar role as helper to others – to earn our worth through service. That way we can maintain control of the situation. But Love is insistent: 'You must sit down … and taste my meat.' This is all too unknown and vulnerable, but Love will have it no other way: 'So I did sit and eat.' There comes a time to change places – a priest must sit and eat. The Eucharist invites receptivity and vulnerability. In praying the Eucharist a priest faces the people and in Christ's person offers bread for life and wine for salvation. But do not turn away from Christ who turns to give you the very same. If it is possible, be a congregation member from time to time. Even if it is not, take pause to allow God to bid you welcome as one who is also in need of this love. For you too need mending, making and strengthening:

> Come my Light, my Feast, my Strength:
> Such a Light, as shows a feast:
> Such a Feast, as mends in length:
> Such a Strength, as makes his guest.[12]

There are always surprises in stepping out of a tradition we have grown up in and opening ourselves to other wisdom. Some years ago I was invited to give a retreat for ministers in the Lutheran Church. According to my Roman Catholic upbringing Luther was the cause of all wrongs. For all my initial nervousness I soon felt at home. What has stayed with me from that retreat was the form of confession and absolution at the beginning of the Eucharist. The people confessed their sins and the priest spoke words of forgiveness; then the priest confessed his failings and the people gave absolution. Whatever the theological nuances between the two traditions the practice spoke to my Catholic heart: we all need a place to own our weakness and we all need another to accept us as the sinner we are.

We are communion. We are – as we hear in the Eucharist – Body of Christ, together rather than in isolation. If one part hurts – priest or congregation member – all hurt with that person; if one part rejoices

---

[12] 'The Call', in *The English Poems of George Herbert*.

then all share in rejoicing. No eye can say to the hand: 'I have no need of you'.[13] The words are familiar and challenging. We depend on one another. We are made for the giving and receiving of the life of the Trinity. No one – and no priest – is exempt.

Experiencing communion

Hopefully there are many opportunities within parish life where priests can experience a genuine sense of belonging and reciprocal care. For those of you reading this book who are not ordained, I urge you to be kind to your priests as people in the same need as anyone else of practical human care and sensitivity. As a young priest I remember sitting in the staff room of the local primary school where I had been visiting the children. It was break time and I was glad of a mug of tea. One teacher looked across at me and said, 'You must be tired.' The words, and the understanding expressed through the eyes that looked upon me, affected me deeply. Someone had seen me, the person, and not just me, the priest. There had been no shortage of smiles and generosity up to that point, but a famine of those who had seen through the outward role to the sometimes struggling human being. Not that I had helped anyone to see that person; I was firmly set in the role of the giver and in no way prepared to receive. In George Herbert's words, love may have to be persistent in its welcome, and priests for their part may need to sit and eat. There will always be questions of appropriate boundaries between those who minister and those they are responsible for. But still, there is room for uncomplicated and insightful kindness, given and received. Communion is not just for worship; it is for living.

Prayer of the Church

I remember the experience of praying morning, evening or night prayer in common at the seminary. For some, morning prayer passed by in the haze of a waking sleep. The performance of night prayer on the one day we were allowed off was sometimes affected by the number of pubs that had been visited. But the words of the psalms

---

[13] 1 Corinthians 12.21.

and the music of the hymns were rich food for the day. This was prayer of the Church and prayer by the Church – an expression of common life, ups and downs, lives intertwined with God and one another.

Praying the Office in the parish was quite a different thing: a solitary task, a jumble of words to somehow get through. It's hard to feel part of a body in such isolation. Isn't it the same with meals? Whatever care is taken, eating alone is a very different experience from eating in company. Food is meant for sharing and conversation. It doesn't taste the same when those we are close to are not present.

In many local churches morning or evening prayer is celebrated in common. Sometimes it is only clergy who meet. A fuller expression of communion is realized by opening up the time of prayer to all. The practice can be hard to establish; numbers who come may be few. In the Catholic tradition for example, historical emphasis has firmly centred on the daily Eucharist; the mould is hard to break. But the Office is also a meal intended for sharing, and once shared it can provide rich food for all: the nurturing word of God *and* an expression and experience of communion. It is worth going the whole way: buying some books, or introducing people to online versions that are often easier to handle. I suggest inviting and preparing people to also take a turn in leading the prayer – or at least part of it; it is another way of breaking down fixed divisions between givers and receivers.

Praying for the Church and the world

Within the Eucharist we hold our world and one another before the goodness of God. Prayers of intercession express a communion that begins in God and, in overflowing, overcomes all boundaries. There are only insiders in the wedding feast between God and humankind.

Priests will often be asked to keep people and situations in their prayers; they will often make the same promise in the course of visiting someone or hearing an account of someone's struggles. To what degree is it possible to be faithful to all the promises of prayer that are made? Where difficulties can arise is if we feel that we must remember each name and every intention to honour the commitment made or, more importantly, for prayer to be effective. God knows their names and needs. When we sit down to pray for people, or as we become aware of their need as we work or walk, the best we can do is to rest them in God's presence and care. Think of the paralysed man let down through the roof into Jesus' presence through the determination of his friends.[14] Sometimes specific words, hopes and desires for the person are forthcoming. At other times it is enough to bring them there before Jesus: a name or a face is enough, with our wishing them good through the goodness of God. And we can also hold anyone who in that moment does not come to mind, for they are in God's mind, and our desire to include them does include them. The Eucharist can also become a way of holding in prayer all those whose lives have touched ours, lifting them to God as bread and wine are offered, raised and blessed. This is what a priest does: intercession flows naturally from the very movements of the liturgy. We do not know – and we certainly cannot control – what the fruit of our prayer is within the lives of those we bring to God. The guiding spirit of our prayer is one of trust and of cooperation with the Holy Spirit.

This movement of active rest in God, expressed in intercession, also shapes the actions and responses of the one who prays. We are faced with situations that need resolution or at least some progress towards a better place. We hope our contact with people will bring good, not harm. Prayer begins to take us out of the realm of anxious interference and towards open and willing cooperation with what God seems to be doing. Prayer for a person, or a problem, or a project begins a process of realignment. When Jesus taught his disciples to pray 'your will be done' he was not suggesting they adopt a spirit of fatalism whereby they renounced any responsibility for what was to come. Instead he was inviting them to orientate their attitudes and actions in willing cooperation with the active desire of God's heart – the God who is always creating, coming alongside, entering into pain and confusion, healing and reconciling. As we have seen, we let go to God in prayer so that we can take hold of life – and our responsibility for people and situations – with our human spirit open to God's Holy Spirit. Prayer takes us into renunciation *and* commitment. What we rest with God are our desires to interfere, fix things quickly but

---

14 Mark 2.1–12.

badly, cling on to control, or win applause. What we seek to take up is God's concern for this person and God's hope at work within this unresolved situation. Prayer begins to shape our responses so that what is done is done together, or as Jesus put it 'you in me and I in you'.[15] It is a natural response – and often a needed one – that we first tell God what to do. We have the answer and God just needs to listen. But the simplicity of the prayer Jesus gave to his disciples encourages us to then let all that go and let God. Trust and cooperation becomes the guiding spirit of prayer and the action that flows from it.

Companions in a common life

> All who believed were together and had all things in common; they would sell their possessions and goods and distribute the proceeds to all, as any had need. Day by day, as they spent much time together in the temple, they broke bread at home and ate their food with glad and generous hearts.[16]

The experience of community can be elusive. Church life, built as it is on the theology and liturgical practice of how we are brought together in communion by God, who is communion, might be the first place we look for it. But it is rarely found or felt there. Worship might bring us together in one place, yet on its own it does not hold us together as true companions – sharers of daily bread. For most congregation members the key focal points of engagement lie elsewhere – in family, workplace or social media networks. Most congregations are too large in number for us to even know one another's names, let alone share what matters in our lives. The local church is rarely as together in mutual commitment as that described in the Acts of the Apostles, and even that congregation was not above falling out over who belonged and what constituted right practice.

Experiences of community do come, often unexpectedly. I remember once getting a strong sense of communion playing football with a group of young people. Our lives were different but the weaving of the ball between us linked us together. Communion was there too

---

[15] John 14.20.
[16] Acts 2.44–46.

in a shared walk through fields and forest in heavy rain – mud and laughter splashed bonds of belonging over all. These are moments of sunlight and glimpses of the kingdom. The taste of community is unmistakable; it is the taste of God.

While in their formation most priests experience features of common life (shared prayer, meals, social time, moaning sessions, times out to have fun), once in a parish priests are often isolated. There are good and generous people around, but the maintenance of appropriate boundaries often puts limits on how far relationships can go. There might be a ministry team or staff team within the church, but for the priest this usually comes with responsibility for oversight. So where do priests go for community? We all need some experience of mutual belonging and sharing. Friendship is food for the spirit, and I will explore its importance and how we make room for it in pages to come. One further possibility is becoming a member of a dispersed, non-residential Christian community such as the Iona Community, the Northumbria Community, the Franciscan Third Order or the Jesus Caritas Fraternity. Commitment to a shared way of life helps to provide the framework for a balanced life centred on God that priesthood by itself lacks. Regular times to meet, pray and talk provide a space for in-depth sharing that may be absent in other settings. Church life does not often allow the connectedness that enables each person to receive what they need to flourish from the proceeds of all; we have to be close enough to notice the needs of another, and develop sufficient trust to own what we lack.

To sustain a ministry centred on communion priests need their own regular experience of community. Where it is lacking we may have to go out and find it. What forms might this take: the regular company of those we can truly call friends; investigating what's involved in belonging to a dispersed religious community; forming our own network of trusted people with whom we can share, pray and laugh together, knowing it is safe to do so? Having found community or chosen where we might seek it, we have to invest time and trust in its development, like those first disciples who made space in their lives to meet, break bread and nurture their communion with one another.

> Those who live according to the flesh set their minds on the things of the flesh, but those who live according to the Spirit set their minds on the things of the Spirit. To set the mind on the flesh is death, but to set the mind on the Spirit is life and peace.[17]

The body has often not been treated well within Christian teaching and writing. In dualistic analyses of the human person the body's raw needs, drives and desires have been framed as enemies of the soul or spirit, with its loftier powers and inclinations. Paul's descriptions of the struggle between God-bound spirit and earth-bound flesh sets the tone (or is undertone?) for attitudes towards our untrustworthy, animal, physical self. Paul himself would not have recognized this disdain for the body. For him the conflict between flesh and spirit was the struggle between desires and reactions moved by self-interest (*sarx*) and those moved by the Holy Spirit, rather than between the Spirit and our physical being (*soma*).

How did we arrive at such a dualistic and confrontational view of the human person, given that the foundation of Christian thought and practice is the Incarnation? Fear of the power of sexual desire was certainly a factor. Perhaps too, we wanted to be able to name what we thought distinguished humankind from the animal world. We can reason, use imagination and exercise the power of free will – the argument went – all qualities of a 'higher' mind than that possessed by 'dumb' animals. The body was a lower, 'base' self, a necessary evil for functioning in this life, naturally inclined towards sin rather than spiritual perfection. The body was a power to control, subdue, ignore and overcome on the path to spiritual freedom. All this even though my quick self-analysis suggests that the mind has much more to answer for in terms of destructive inclination and behaviour!

I hope you are of a generation that escaped the worst of this naming of the body as unclean. As the voice of Peter's dream put it, 'what God has made clean you must not call profane'.[18] Disdain for the body cannot be reconciled with affirmation of the Incarnation.

---

[17] Romans 8.5–6.
[18] Acts 10.15.

Jesus meets us in the body; he joins us in hunger, thirst, delight, desire and beating of the heart:

> We declare to you what was from the beginning, what we have heard, what we have seen with our eyes, what we have looked at and touched with our hands.[19]

Jesus' teaching and ministry have such a physical quality about them. He speaks about people who work with their hands: farmers and fishermen, women who make bread. God cares, he says, about blades of grass, the smallest of sparrows and hairs on the head. He heals through the touch of his hands and the spittle from his mouth. He overturns tables, washes feet and prepares loaves and fish on a fire for breakfast. He is plunged into water and jostled by crowds. He feels the desperate touch of a lonely, sick woman. Thirsty after long, hot journeying, he asks a Samaritan woman for a drink. He offers his wounded body to the touch of his doubting disciple. It is impossible to separate Jesus' teaching from the physicality of his being or the world he grew up in, marvelled at and loved.

The liturgy of the Church into which priests are flung reflects this physicality. We mark transitional points on the Christian journey with tangible signs: water we are washed in, oil that anoints our bodies, bread and wine we share together, rings we place on one another's fingers, the laying on of hands. We name ourselves together 'the Body of Christ'. In our different traditions we vary in the ways we use the body to express prayer, yet share the same physical language of communication: we raise hands in praise, or make a sign of the cross; we lay on hands in prayer for healing or light a candle to express our desires. In a more Catholic tradition there is perhaps greater ease in using colour, scent or action within worship but all traditions of worship are embodied in some way. How else could it be?

Priestly ministry celebrates incarnation, but to what degree is the body honoured in the daily life of a priest? Is it sometimes no more than the willing, or unwilling, workhorse that is dragged along without much care or attention? How do we give the body the respect it is due? Priestly ministry celebrates incarnation, but how far is this

---

[19] 1 John 1.1.

reflected in the variety of ways we express our prayer? Do we see our needy, demanding bodies as obstacles, or means to communion with God? How can we pray with the body rather than despite it?

Honouring the body

One of Francis of Assisi's early biographers, Thomas of Celano, tells of a conversation between Francis and one of his brothers about care of the body.[20] Francis had a long history of treating what he called 'Brother Ass' badly. He endured long periods of fasting, wore the poorest of garments even when it was bitterly cold and neglected to look after himself when he was unwell – all in the quest to overcome any selfish desire that might get in the way of giving himself completely to the love and service of Christ. Francis became physically exhausted and seriously ill. Still he hesitated to look after his urgent bodily needs through rest, better food and medication. Was it right that he should do so? He asked advice from the other brother. 'When your body was able, did it serve you faithfully?' the unnamed brother asked. Francis confessed that his body had served him well and given him all that it was able. 'Well then,' the brother replied, 'where is your generosity? Where is your discernment? If you accept favours from a friend who serves you so well, why would you not show kindness when that same friend is in such need?' Francis recognized he had been in the wrong and repented: 'Cheer up Brother Body, and forgive me, for I will now gladly do as you please.'

This latter-day conversion came too late to save Francis' life, but it was still a significant reconciliation. There had been – as the brother pointed out – a generosity gap in Francis' life. He honoured Brother Sun, Mother Earth and Sister Moon. He never hesitated to give anything he had to a person in need. His body – the 'Ass' – was the only one denied a place in the family, condemned instead to be a slave until, at the last, he was welcomed as a true brother.

Most of us do not go out of our way to intentionally mistreat our body. But do we honour the body as a faithful friend? How generous

---

20 Thomas of Celano, in Regis J. Armstrong, J. A. Wayne Hellman and William J. Short (eds), 2000, *The Founder: Volume 2 of Francis of Assisi: Early Documents*, London: New City Press, 'Second Book of Thomas of Celano', chapter CLX.

are we in the body's time of need? As a man, and a celibate man, and someone in any case predisposed to be as mean as they come towards personal needs, the die was cast that my body would suffer. Every post-Christmas break was celebrated with a bout of illness. My teeth still regret the lack of care shown them during those years. Hopefully you have more going for you in regard to respecting the body than I did.

But I wonder how often the needs of the body are put on hold when the pressure of work mounts. When push comes to shove it is often the body that must do the shoving. Those involved in pastoral care are often neglectful of their own needs. Physical breakdowns of health offer a warning; but it might take more than one before we start to take notice. The body is a brother or sister – not a slave or a machine.

Balance and the body

> Give me neither poverty nor riches;
> feed me with the food that I need.[21]

In the West we are all in a muddle about care for the body. Everything is available and instant and this doesn't always serve us. The rhythms of work and rest that once flowed with night and darkness no longer need apply. The ability to do most things by a click of the finger doesn't bode well for all the other muscles in the body that need regular exercise to maintain their vitality. While the hungry are still in our midst, more people struggle with eating too much or relying on ready-prepared foods that lack the nutrients the body needs. Some join a gym and others go vegan. These can be valid individual responses to the crisis that has crept up on us. However, true conversion also reaches down to the level of our attitudes and beliefs. Is our body a 'thing' we can use or abuse, or is our body a sister or brother – and all we are? We have no life beyond it. Theologically, the body is holy: the temple of the Spirit and the breathing place of Christ. For priests, as witnesses of the incarnation, reverence for the body is proper matter for preaching and living.

One of the enduring qualities of the *Rule of Saint Benedict* is its

---

[21] Proverbs 30.8.

careful attention to balance. There are proper times to work and rest and neither must be disregarded. Physical labour is as honourable and important as mental exercise.[22] Clothing is distributed according to the needs of the season and the climate, and should fit the wearer.[23] Those who are sick should be given the rest, care and food necessary to aid their recovery.[24] Two kinds of cooked food should be available so that each individual's needs are met. In times of heavy work more food can be given. Overindulgence is to be avoided, not least because the body itself suffers.[25]

Talk of clothing, food, sleep and work might seem mundane in a 'spiritual' text, but for Benedict proper attention to the needs of the body is vital to Christian discipleship. One of the guiding principles of the Rule is reverence: the stranger is holy and is to be welcomed as if Christ;[26] all the utensils and goods of the monastery are to be treated in the same way as the sacred vessels of the altar;[27] the body is to be honoured as holy and God-given. The balance in Benedict's Rule is more than self-help advice or the latest health-kick; it is theology of incarnation in practice.

Reviewing our relationship with our body

The above heading might immediately transport us to that uneasy moment when we first gaze at ourselves in the mirror in the morning. Sometimes the information given then can be useful; more often than not it leads us to dislike the body even more. The mirror we need is a greater one, able to help us reflect on our attitudes towards our physical wellbeing and our respect for this bodily self that is made in the image of God.

The review we make of the way we relate to our body is best made in the context of prayer, in trust that God loves us more than we do and desires our good.

---

[22] *The Rule of Saint Benedict,* Chapter 48.
[23] *Benedict,* Chapter 55.
[24] *Benedict,* Chapter 36.
[25] *Benedict,* Chapter 39.
[26] *Benedict,* Chapter 53.
[27] *Benedict,* Chapter 31.

- Do I get enough rest?
- How well do I eat?
- Does my body have sufficient opportunity to exercise?
- Do I honour my body as a brother or sister, or abuse it as a slave or a machine?
- As I reflect with God about the above, what sense do I have of any practical way I might honour my body?

What comes from such a prayerful review will be shaped to us as individuals. Listen well. Perhaps the answers come in a crowd; but is there one response among these that might begin the process of honouring the body? It usually works better to have a single focus than trying to make several changes at once.

For what it's worth here are some fruits from my own reflection. They may help you begin to imagine what is beneficial for you – but these will not be your answers.

I honour my body when

- I make time to walk each day
- I work in the garden
- I get up and do something else if I have been working at my desk for too long
- I go to bed when I am tired rather than fall asleep in front of the television
- I eat food that has colour and variety rather than go for the quickest option
- I enjoy a drink but I avoid over-consumption
- I make space to use all my senses in being present to what is around me
- I take time to swim in the sea once it becomes warm enough.

Sometimes we look inside the mind for an answer to what we need when it is the body that can help us. I remember my first experience of the wonders of digging. I was at seminary and had a good deal on my mind. A group was asked (told?) to move some earth from one place to another. I have no idea why and am not even sure that there was any good purpose. But I dug. As time went on the rhythm of digging began to ease my inner tension. At the end of an hour I was physically tired but inwardly relaxed in a way I hadn't been for some time. I am not recommending that you go and buy yourself a spade as the cure for all ills. But if you listen to it, your body might have an answer to what you deep down need.

Honour the body. It is in the nature of priesthood to do so.

Praying with the body

Within the Eucharist in particular a priest prays through the body: extending the arms in prayer to God; signing blessing in a cross-shaped movement of the hands; sharing peace through embrace. The actions of offering, taking, blessing and sharing bread and wine embody the prayer of Christ's living and dying, rising and reconciling, uniting and sending. As a congregation we stand, kneel or sit in rhythm with the different movements of the liturgy. More than a gathering of words the Eucharist is a prayer of the body.

In my earliest memory of being taught to pray at school, the body played its full part: hands were to be placed together and eyes closed as lips moved. Entering church I was to bend my knee. Making myself ready to greet God I signed the cross on forehead, heart and shoulders. As Teresa of Avila protested when urged to put aside all thought – even of Christ – in the place of prayer, 'we are not angels ... we have a body'.[28] We too are words from God made flesh. Incarnation is our reality and our place of encounter.

However, for the most part we do not consider the place of the body within our prayer. We tend to focus on the workings of our mind as if that is where the real stuff is happening. The body's posture might help but that's as far as we generally go. And yet, in communication the movement of the body and the voicing of words work together – not apart. Take for example, the way we use our hands.

I speak with my hands. I use my voice too, but my hands do a great deal of talking. One day my wife, June, was present when I was leading a day on ways of prayer. The person sitting next to her asked if I was 'signing'. I have no knowledge of British Sign Language

---

[28] Kieran Kavanagh and Otilio Rodriguez, 1976, *The Collected Works of Teresa of Avila*, Washington D.C: ICS Publications, Volume One, 'The Book of Her Life' 22.10.

or any equivalent system; it's just that my hands will not be still – their movements are an integral part of my self-expression. I am not alone in this. Recently I sat outside St Pancras station, getting some air while I waited for my train. Though I was out of earshot of the people passing by on the way towards the platforms, I could sense something of their conversation through the gestures of their hands: a 'hurry up' issued through the urgent beckoning of fingers; a 'good to be with you' impressed by one hand joining with another, the telling and receiving of an adventure made alive through the busy work of hands moving up, down and around.

In the normal course of conversation we hardly notice how much is said with our hands. We hear the voice, and later in the day it is words we can recall. And yet in the moment the movement of our hands expresses what we hold within and desire to share. If you are not sure this is so, I suggest you watch television with the sound turned off; it will still be full of 'speech'. Sometimes the movements of the body reveal what remains hidden by the spoken word: the speaker's ease or lack of it; their frustration, or joy, or fear.

Without knowing it to be so, I wonder whether signing preceded vocal communication in human history. Even now when faced with a language barrier we turn to our hands to attempt to express what words cannot convey. Signing with the hands remains an established part of our social exchanges. We shake hands as a way of greeting, clap hands to express our appreciation, stretch out our open hands to communicate our welcome. A policeman puts out his hand, palm outwards, to stop the traffic. Beyond this socially agreed language, our inmost feelings find voice in the shaping of our hands. When we are tense or angry we may curl our fingers into tight balls or fold our hands across our body. When making a point I notice how my downwards moving hand meets my upwards facing palm at right angles: the two connect. In excitement or wonder, hands wander upwards and outwards.

I also have a sense that the reshaping of hands can alter what is happening at the level of our attitudes or feelings. Just as the mind finds expression in the body, the body can help the mind into a new place. There I am sitting in the place of prayer. My hands stretch out, upwards facing, the fingers curled to receive what I need, or to offer what I have. What is expressed in the body begins to find a way into my spirit.

So when you next find space to listen to the longings of your heart, let your hands lead you into prayer. No words are needed. Your hands will know what it is your deepest self seeks.

The body knows the moves

'We played the flute for you and you did not dance.'[29]

Today at the Eucharist the priest led the children present in praying the 'Our Father' with song and movement. Some adults joined in too; most hung back, or like me self-consciously raised a hand here or there, all the time wary of the reactions of neighbours. Though we have choreographed movement within the Eucharist (standing, kneeling, or shaking hands) outside this most of us are reluctant movers. Perhaps it's a British thing; we are not the most demonstrative of people. It might also reflect received expectations about remaining orderly in church: we move, but only when the sergeant-major tells us to.

You may come from a tradition where ease of movement is more acceptable. For some years I was part of charismatic prayer group and despite my inhibitions I dared to raise my hands in praise, and speak in tongues with the rest. Whatever our received tradition and upbringing I believe that the body presses to help our spirit to pray. I think of people in the very different context of silent retreats who feel moved in a moment to curl into a ball, or lie flat on the ground, or dance on a mountain top. There are moments when words, or the workings of the mind, have to give way to the body; the body alone knows the moves of our spirit and God's Spirit.

Suggestions for prayer

Choose a different physical position for prayer
In the *Spiritual Exercises* Ignatius Loyola suggests a variety of possible bodily positions for prayer:

---

[29] Matthew 11.17.

I will enter upon the meditation, now kneeling, now prostrate upon the ground, now lying face upwards, now seated, now standing.[30]

It is worth exploring whether a change of bodily stance might help express different movements within your prayer. Perhaps walking works well for you when you are reflecting on the day with God. On a particular day, lying face upwards might help carry your heartfelt desire to open your life to the movement of the Spirit. Listen to what your body tells you. Ignatius suggests that if a particular posture helps you in the moment then stay with it. In other words, don't use restless shifting about as a way of avoiding prayer.

Use physical action as a way of stilling oneself before God

I will show you how I do not cease praying, simply by going on with my work. I am there sitting in God's presence. And when I put my little leaves to soak and when I start to weave a rope I say: 'Have mercy on me, Lord, according to your steadfast love' (Psalm 51.1). Is not that a prayer?[31]

People who knit are often good listeners. The repetitive physical movement creates a more centred and attentive space within. The body begins to still the restless movement of the mind. I notice the same effect as I carry out routine gardening tasks: raking fallen leaves, gathering fruit or extracting seeds from the dried husks of their pods. You may notice that you are more relaxed when you are ironing or making bread. If the body naturally carries you into a greater stillness in one of these ways then use this activity to pray. Knead the dough in God's company; iron out your restlessness; knit attentive openness to the Spirit. All that might be needed is your choice in that activity to seek God and perhaps a prayer phrase or chant to say or sing as and when you need.

---

[30] Louis J. Puhl SJ, 1951, *The Spiritual Exercises of St. Ignatius: Based on studies in the language of the autograph*, Chicago: Loyola University Press. Exx 76.

[31] Lucius, *Patrologia Graeca*, Migne 65,253, quoted in Olivier Clement, 1997, *The Roots of Christian Mysticism*, 4th edn, London: New City, p. 203.

Attentiveness to the body as a way of moving into a receptive space before God

Where you are now is a meeting place with God. Whether you are travelling on a crowded train, sitting in the kitchen at home or kneeling in a church pew, God is here and now.

Turn aside to welcome this presence.

You can begin by becoming aware of this meeting place, this 'here' and 'now' moment by moving from the busy flow of your thoughts into your senses.

Listen to the sounds of this place, giving all your attention to your hearing: louder sounds and quieter; from close by and from distant places; with different tones and textures.

Look at what is around you: the shapes and the colours, the light and the shadow. Take time to gaze; this is a deep breath between all that activity, and God is in this deep breath.

As you stay in this meeting place you may become aware of your physical self: the weight of your feet on the floor, the relaxation of your fingers as you let them uncurl, the slow rhythm of your breathing. Be present to yourself in this way, for God meets you here.

Your feeling self may also greet you: the lightness or heaviness, tiredness or energy, gratitude or sorrow. Receive your feeling self gently, as a guest in this place. A name for how you feel in this moment may come to you. Acknowledge its presence with you but also let it go; allow it to rest.

In this meeting place your thoughts will come and go. They might want to hustle you out of this moment, telling you there's somewhere more important you need to be. But there's nowhere more important for this moment than here and now – where God is. Even hurry and worry deserve to rest for a while.

When your mind is overactive, let your body still you into quiet attentiveness.

Herald of the Gospel

How beautiful upon the mountains are the feet of the messenger who announces peace, who brings good news, who announces salvation, who says to Zion, 'Your God reigns.'[32]

Easter lies at the heart of the Christian year. For priests the pressure is on: a series of complex liturgies; a building to turn from stark emptiness to flowering beauty in a matter of days; people to find to help celebrate the mystery. But no feast is fuller of meaning and relevance. Easter is hope realized, reality transformed. The paschal season makes sense of us as people, as Christians and as disciples. The pain of Good Friday and the loss of the Saturday that follows gather all our struggles and confusions. The remembrance of those days holds our hurts and the wounds of all those we have come alongside, listened to, and felt inadequate before. The events of that first Easter morning take nothing away from what has taken place. There is darkness, and it is real, but into it comes unimagined light. Christ is risen, and all creation rises in him. Every chain that holds us in death is broken.

As I listen to the readings of the Easter Vigil I hear the story of a people, and I hear our own stories. We are created, cast into slavery, set free, driven into exile and brought back into our own land. We wait and long for what is not yet present. We are given a way to live that we consistently fail to follow. We are promised living water and it breaks unexpectedly from the rock of our experiences. The fire is lit, the candles burn. A new song, an *Exsultet*, announces the dawn. Hearing the story of salvation afresh I realize that each of us has a good news story told within the pages of our lives. The work of a priest lies in this: to proclaim the Easter mystery and to invite us to recognize and trust the truth of this gospel within the brokenness and confusion of our past and current experience.

Every priest, whatever their tradition, is called to be an evangelist. They are to share the good news they continue to receive and are being transformed by. This is more than doctrine out of a textbook; it is the

---

[32] Isaiah 52.7.

story of a life. What is the shape and form of your gospel? Where have you seen the footprints of Christ? When have you sensed his touch? How did he call you to himself? How does he call you now? Amid the demands of priestly ministry it is easy to lose touch with your own unique story of salvation – incomplete though it is.

I sometimes wonder whether each priest has only one message to share. That seems ridiculous given the different themes of teaching and preaching they will cover in a lifetime of ministry. But often one thread comes through, weaving in and out of whatever is the subject at hand. I recognize this in myself: I speak about a God of compassionate and accepting presence who labours to free us from all that hinders us from realizing our God-given being, and invites our cooperation. It is what I know; it is my gospel. I have not fully comprehended it for myself; it is still soaking in. But I feel compelled to share it. What is your gospel? How does it flow from your story?

Speaking your word

> May you come to realize what that word is, the message of Jesus that God wants to speak to the world by your life. Let yourself be transformed. Let yourself be renewed by the Spirit, so that this can happen.[33]

If each of us is a word of God then we evangelize not only through what we say or write but by consenting to the Spirit's work of drawing us into the truth of our being. Here once more is the importance of our openness to God. We have a word of life to proclaim, and only God can help us speak it. There is one common Gospel and one shared Creed; and each of us has a gospel, and in our actions we profess our personal creed. The universal and the particular illuminate one another. The active-passive tone of Pope Francis' words is telling: 'let yourself be transformed … let yourself be renewed'. The choice each one of us faces is whether or not we dare allow God the room to go on creating and naming us. Evangelists must be people of prayer; only silence before God gives birth to words of God.

---

[33] Pope Francis: *Gaudete et exsultate* 24.

A word of hope

At the heart of evangelism is hope. Hope has nothing in common with the kind of wishful thinking that seeks escape from reality. Hope is always in the real and actual, for this is where God is. How do we allow such hope to seep down into the roots of our sometimes awkward and unwanted reality? We can hold on to the theology – and so we must; it is the testimony of generations past. But it is often the small details of a day or the prolonged wear and tear of our circumstances that challenge our capacity for hope. Perhaps the car breaks down, or we hurt our back, or the project we put so much into comes to nothing. Perhaps a vital meeting goes on too long and then ends badly. Where is hope in these so small settings that hold neither glamour nor glory? It is not tied to particular outcomes. Our hope rests in never being abandoned; its source lies in the endless persistence and resourcefulness of the love of God that continues to flow through the bad day and the difficult encounter. As the prophet Habakkuk professed:

> Though the fig tree does not blossom, and no fruit is on the vines; though the produce of the olive fails and the fields yield no food … yet I will rejoice in the Lord; I will exult in the God of my salvation.[34]

Working as a priest, responding to the difficulties of others while negotiating the complexities of one's own personality, there are times when the fig tree fails to blossom; hard work doesn't always bring the fruit it deserves. Once more we are there at the start of Holy Week and not yet at Easter. But somewhere, even amid this dark, a spark of fire is burning; and though we may not now see it, we know the light is coming. Being alongside people in a place of pain and confusion there is no place for empty, easy platitudes. Our hope often has no words, but it finds form in staying there and not turning away. Without our knowing it, and within the experience of our inadequacy, we may be for another that small glimmer of brightness that hints – just hints – at the possibility of day. Every Eucharist plunges a priest into the depths of this mystery. Every sign of the cross made is a pledge of

---

[34] Habakkuk 3.17–18.

Easter hope. Every funeral a priest conducts faces them with death that is all too real and yet is transparent to life. Hope is baptism of immersion; we do not turn from the overwhelming water but instead seek its depths where life is well hidden.

The Good News of Jesus

Jesus Christ is the same yesterday and today and for ever.[35]

As a Catholic I grew up bowing my head every time the name of Jesus was spoken. Given I went to a Catholic primary school and a Catholic church I did a good deal of bowing. Statues and pictorial representations of Jesus served to both draw and distance me from him. Here was a compelling figure with all-seeing eyes and visible marks of holiness. By these same features he was not like me. You don't get too close to someone you have to bow to. When I started to read the New Testament the person of Jesus began to put on human flesh and bones. My imagination came into play. I could see Jesus walking on the water or healing a man blind from birth. I wanted to be there and be part of that story. Jesus began to move out of past time into my time. Then – at a moment of crisis – Jesus came out of the history books into the very place where I was. I could sense his presence and, more than this, the warmth of his acceptance of me. This became the good news I wanted to share. Ordination training followed, and within it, for the first time, some biblical studies. I remember my disturbance when it was suggested that Jesus, being fully human, would not have known for certain what was to come. The doubts of Jesus were real; his knowledge and understanding grew as ours does. I was not prepared for this humble manifestation of God in a shared humanity. I was more comfortable keeping him at some distance as the hero figure, removed from our uncertainties and the match of every circumstance. But as I came to see, this vulnerability was the very best of news. His journey and my journey were interwoven rather than separate. There was no place I could go where he was not.

How did the Jesus of the Gospels enter your story? Who is Jesus for you now? As the writer of the letter to the Hebrews states, he is

---

[35] Hebrews 13.8.

yesterday, today and for ever. Though located at a point of time and space, this presence – and all it expresses of who God is and who we are – transcends theses horizons. As Mark understands, the good news *is* Jesus Christ.[36] Evangelism has its source in gazing at Jesus and pondering his actions, attitudes and words. Reading the Gospels is one way we do this, but as the practice of *lectio divina* suggests, 'reading' by itself is not enough: we have to allow room for the sights and sounds of the Gospels to soak down to our roots. There is also a necessary movement across time and space, allowing this life to touch and transform what is happening for us now.

One practice I have found helpful in allowing the Gospels to be in conversation with our experience is what is sometimes called 'imaginative contemplation'. Ignatius Loyola made liberal use of this way of prayer within the *Spiritual Exercises*. Using the imagination we bring the events of the Gospels from the past into the present and place ourselves within the scene. Thus, when contemplating the birth of Jesus, Ignatius suggests we imagine the road from Nazareth to Bethlehem. Rather than tell us what the road is like, he invites us to consider whether the way is level, or through hills and valleys; it might be narrow or broad. The cave where Jesus is born might be large or small, high or low. He encourages us to see the people there without telling us in detail what they look like. The imagination is given free rein. Then he asks us to enter the scene and find our place there and 'as though present' look upon them and serve them.[37] Ignatius believed engaging with the Gospels in this way would help us come to 'an intimate knowledge of our Lord' and move us to 'love him more and follow him more closely'.[38] The point of the practice is not to prove how vivid our imagination is, but to draw us deeper into discipleship. Jesus' actions and words begin to address us. He enters into our fears, hopes and longings. The encounter invites a response from us, or helps us see more clearly how Jesus meets us in this place. Imaginative contemplation is perhaps most helpful in the context Ignatius envisaged – namely an individually guided retreat – where there is opportunity to explore with one's guide the experience of

---

[36] Mark 1.1.
[37] Puhl, *Spiritual Exercises*, Exx 111–117.
[38] Exx 104.

prayer. What did I notice? What did I feel? Why did my imagination take me the way it did? What light does this give to my understanding of the movement of the Spirit in my life?

Even if we do not use this means of prayer in a formal sense, the imagination has a place in our engagement with the person of Jesus. Because he is yesterday, today and for ever, he is always present, and we are there among the band of followers who take the road with him to Jerusalem, who gaze in dismay as his life ebbs away, and hear him speak peace in a room where the doors are locked. We too can declare the good news of 'what we have seen with our eyes, what we have looked at and touched with our hands'.[39]

Remembering wonders of old

I will call to mind the deeds of the Lord;
I will remember your wonders of old.[40]

Through the proclamation of the Gospel, the recitation of the Creed and the sharing of the eucharistic feast, a priest awakens faith in the present activity of God through the remembrance of our shared salvation history. We look back to gain a stance to look forward. The turning of liturgical seasons draws us into the timeless generosity of God. The *kerygma* of the early Church announced the fulfilment of earthly longings through the birth, ministry, death and resurrection of Jesus and the outpouring of the Holy Spirit. We draw from memory to share what is alive in the present moment.

Alongside the witness of our shared Christian story, remembering our personal journey with God helps us gain a firmer footing as we seek to go forward into a future we cannot wholly see or manage. Many of us will have been asked to write about, or describe, the story of the development of our faith as part of the selection process for ordination. As we did so, scattered events began to join up to make a connected narrative. Like the disciples on the road to Emmaus, telling our story has a revelatory power of its own. If we feel lost and confused in our current circumstances, remembering puts us back in touch with the orientation that has carried us thus far and with

---

[39] 1 John 1.1.
[40] Psalm 77.11.

the God who summoned us to make this journey. What if – once each year – we set aside a day to tell our own story once more? As we do so Jesus walks with us, unravelling the strange scriptures of our experience. Each year's remembering will be different, for we will have reached a new place. Some of what was unknown will have fallen into place, and other mysteries and questions will have come to the surface. But when we can put particular events and stirrings in the larger context of our salvation history we are more able to have faith that, though much remains unclear, there is purpose and direction in our travelling. It might help to choose a day and go to a place that holds personal significance for us. It will be a day of pilgrimage – actual or symbolic. There may be someone – or a group – you want to share this day with: those who have journeyed most closely with you.

An alternative might be to walk a prayer labyrinth. As you move inwards, remember the road you have travelled. When you reach the centre, pause to take in where you now are. As you leave the centre and move outwards, put what is unknown and unclear in God's hands. Let go to God any way you sense your path might now lead you.

Giving thanks

> O give thanks to the Lord, for he is good;
> for his steadfast love endures for ever.[41]

The Eucharist reminds us to give thanks. 'Thank you' is the simplest yet most powerful of prayers. Gratitude grounds us in relationship. All that we receive and everything that gladdens our heart is a gift of God. Our heart becomes lighter and the day less dark. There will be difficulties in our day, and often pain or sorrow too. 'Thank you' does not deny the existence of our struggles, but we recognize we are not alone in facing them. Thanksgiving makes us aware of the wonder of small things: the excitement of a child, the singing of a blackbird or the taste of fresh bread. And even if no birds sing, steadfast love continues to keep us. I doubt it is possible to be an evangelist of a generous God without the joy that wakens through giving thanks. I also believe that God thanks us for our generosity; the relationship goes both ways.

---

[41] Psalm 107.1.

An evangelist proclaims not just news but *good* news. This good news does not always conform to our ideas about wanted outcomes. The message of those who promise material prosperity and popular acclaim in return for obedience to their pastors rings hollow. The Cross remains part of our Gospel and experience. We still mark the Friday of Jesus' death and we call it 'Good', for here amid suffering is the one who is life for us. Our joy is not rooted in events going our way but in God going our way – whatever that journey entails. This is the Gospel we share: the good news of Jesus Christ. In this Gospel Jesus shares with us his joy and makes our joy complete.[42]

---

[42] John 15.11.

6

Rain for Roots:
The Priest as Friend

With your own place to shelter

> For you have been a refuge to the poor,
> a refuge to the needy in their distress,
> a shelter from the rainstorm and a shade from the heat.
> When the blast of the ruthless was like a winter rainstorm,
> the noise of aliens like heat in a dry place,
> you subdued the heat with the shade of clouds;
> the song of the ruthless was stilled.[1]

Priesthood is by its nature a public ministry: so public that sometimes, as Jesus found, there is no place to lay one's head. And yet Jesus did seek and find shelter. Martha opened her home to him.[2] In the early morning hours, while it was still dark, he 'got up and went out to a deserted place', where he prayed.[3] When evening came and the crowds went home, he sat, ate and talked with those who knew him best. They demanded no sign to justify his actions. He could be Jesus, a son of a carpenter and their companion along the road.

We all need a shelter from the rainstorm and shade from the heat. Jesus found his refuge in places where he could be by himself, in people who accepted him as he was and in times of the day that were for his own resourcing. Shelter and shade found in places, people and time: in the summer heat and the winter rain priests need their refuge too.

---

[1] Isaiah 25.4–5.
[2] Luke 10.35.
[3] Mark 1.35.

Places

A change of place can signify to oneself – and to other people – that now I step out of availability into my own refuge. I once visited a woman who was training to become an authorized pastoral care volunteer in her diocese. At the end of the conversation she invited me to come out of the house and into her small courtyard garden. She opened the door of a shed and asked me to follow her in. A little wary now, I entered in. Instead of the usual jungle of garden tools, unwanted furniture and tins of half-used paint I found myself in a cosy sitting room, furnished with comfortable seating, colourful rugs, and cushions. In one corner was an icon, a candle and a vase of fresh cut flowers. 'Here is where I come to sit, read and pray', she explained, 'the children know that when I am in here I am not to be disturbed and they leave me alone.' She had made her refuge and been determined about it. It was her space, and no children, tools or junk belonged inside.

It might take that level of grit and clarity to make a refuge where you live: be it shed or attic or prayer room. It will not be a forever place to hide from responsibility – she had her children and her work and she gave herself generously to both. But the creation and sustaining of a physical space such as this makes a statement to us and to others: to function well, and to go on responding to the needs of those we care for, our soul needs its own familiar shelter. A place of refuge can take forms other than a room at home. When I worked in a parish in south-east London I often walked to Greenwich Park. It was helpful for me to sometimes get out of crowded streets with their limited horizons. I needed big skies, green trees and comfortable anonymity. In latter days, working in Borough High Street, I sought out Red Cross Gardens a short walk away, where I could lose myself in gazing at the pond, or sit for a while on the grass with my back against a tree. I might only be there for 15 minutes, but the familiarity of the setting immediately moved me to a different interior space. I was no longer 'at work', 'on duty'.

A retreat house can also become a known place of refuge. With regular visits, it takes less time to switch into what the house offers: quiet, places to sit or walk, an invitation to reflect, or simply to be with

God. Just as, when a child, I associated closing my eyes and putting hands together with prayer, entry into the physical surroundings of the retreat house becomes an invitation to let our empty bucket down into the well of the Spirit. There can be more surprising places that link us with our deepest self and with God: an art gallery, perhaps, or a cafe where amid the buzz of unknown voices we find a hospitable place to be. For one priest I spoke to, St Pancras International station had become her cathedral where she walked on holy ground. The Bible is full of such places of encounter: a bush in the desert, the bank of a river, a marketplace or a city garden. Perhaps the place chooses us, if we stop to listen. Where do I feel more myself? Where do I easily sense God with me? Where am I at ease?

Last but not necessarily least among these places of refuge is the church building itself. For most priests it is on the doorstep – or at least, often visited. For so many people within and beyond recognized faith communities, an open church is an invitation: somewhere wide and high enough to receive whatever it is I am feeling or going through; somewhere that doesn't ask me to be anything else other than the person I am. If the door is open, those who need the space most will find their way in. Does the church building become so familiar to priests that they fail to recognize the gift that it is? In this house of prayer all are welcomed. Find yourself a corner and make yourself at home there. Interruption is possible, but for the most part people respect whoever is seeking silence and peace, layperson or priest.

People

> Do not press me to leave you
> or to turn back from following you!
> Where you go, I will go;
> where you lodge, I will lodge;
> your people shall be my people,
> and your God my God.[4]

Naomi felt her life had come to an end. Her husband and sons had died. There was famine in the land; she was far from home and

---

[4] Ruth 1.16.

further from hope. She resolved to travel back to her home town, Bethlehem, and called her two daughters-in-law to her to thank them for their kindness and send them away. But Ruth would not leave her, joined as they were by shared grief and bonds of love. Ruth became the shelter for Naomi's sorrow until the day she conceived a child and both their lives were restored. The trajectory of the story leads towards the eventual reign of David, Ruth's great-grandson; this is the larger narrative. But here the small stands immense: the unbreakable friendship between two women of different generations and nationalities who lead each other towards unexpected happiness.

Which story matters more in the life of a priest? The difference they make to people in their congregation and the life of the parish, or those bonds of deep relationship where shelter has been offered and found? Or is this a false question based on the presumption of a necessary competition between the two? In the story of Ruth and Naomi the small detail of the qualities of their relationship became the larger picture of the future of a nation: the two strands cannot be separated.

Losing touch

In my years as a priest I began to lose touch with my closest friends. In part this was because I had not learned yet that friendships need to be nurtured: there are only so many people we meet in life who can be that unconditional shelter for us, and we for them. I also lost contact because I became too enmeshed in the all-encompassing work of being a priest and being available. I did not set aside enough time or mental space to be with those who knew me best and loved me for myself. Where choices came, I favoured my 'vocation'. In my actions – if not always consciously – I chose God over my own needs, parishioners over friends. The truth is more complex: in choosing 'God' I was also opting for what gave me a sense of purpose and worth. Was it God or was it me I was choosing? When – after leaving the priesthood – I married, I still faced the same question. My sense of vocation was undiminished. So what would come first: the work that expressed this sense of calling or the most important person in my life? Looking back I recognize I often did the same thing: took for granted that those deep relationships were there and would look after themselves; the more pressing matter was my work.

I wonder how typical my story is. Being a priest carries such weight of purpose, with no less than God presumed to be behind it. For those in the Catholic tradition celibacy seems to imply that mere earthly relationships must fall second to the work of God. Even for those priests who have partners and children the power of a call that appears to put God first can create real tension between different areas of responsibility. But while in one moment of time we can be pulled in two opposing directions and forced to make a choice between the two, I now wonder whether this larger picture of competition between the call of God and humankind is a false one. For what is being a priest but serving a God who calls us into relationship? Love of God and neighbour are not two different loves. We learn to love God, and to allow ourselves to be loved by God, by allowing another to love us and draw us out of self-interest in loving them. And where better to learn love than with friends, partners or children? The vocation of a priest embraces the love of human beings; there are not two vocations, but one.

The friendship of Christ

'I do not call you servants any longer, because the servant does not know what the master is doing; but I have called you friends, because I have made known to you everything I have heard from my Father.'[5]

Aelred, a monk of the Cistercian community at Rievaulx, wrote of how the qualities of human friendship not only reflect the love of God but lead us into that love. For Aelred, we have many relationships, but few that allow our spirit to rest: where we can freely and safely pour out our souls.[6] He believed that while we are called to love all, friendship was a rare and precious gift. For him, a friend was one who could not but love you, who held your secrets and had the space to

---

[5] John 15.15.
[6] Aelred of Rievaulx (1109–67), *Mirror of Charity* 3.39.

receive your pain and joy. For Aelred, the faithfulness and generosity of friends was a true mirror of the love of God.[7]

We receive and share the life of God through friendship. We need friends – and they need us – because we need God. Aelred's understanding of the particular qualities of friendship is important. The term is used too freely within social media. We have many unequal relationships where one consistently leans heavily on the other. There are people whose company we enjoy but who we would not trust with what is important to us. We have responsibilities within these relationships, but these are not our friends. A friend is a safe shelter – or rather friends are safe shelters for one another. Where we have them, we must treasure them. Time spent with friends may well be going to the cinema together, meeting up for a drink or some sightseeing on a day off; the outwardly 'secular' nature of what is shared does not negate how this time with friends can also keep us in the love of God.

There will often be difficulties in the way of friendship between a priest and someone in their congregation. Other eyes look to see whether this person is shown special favour. There can be questions of boundaries: do both parties understand the relationship in the same way? There will be limits on what can be shared. All of which is not to say that such friendship is impossible, but that equality of relationship and depth of sharing can be challenging to hold. Often those friends who are one step removed and yet close to us are more helpful. You may have friends who knew you before you set out to be a priest and do not view you through that lens. They call you by name. Such space can be liberating; it can help remind us of who we are beyond our responsibilities.

The key people in our lives – our friends, our partner or our children – do not stand in the way of our vocation. They are also our vocation. If we can learn to be loved and to love within these relationships we will receive and share the love that God is.

---

[7] Aelred, *Spiritual Friendship* 3.6.

> Some people brought a blind man to him and begged him to touch him. He took the blind man by the hand and led him out of the village; and when he had put saliva on his eyes and laid his hands on him, he asked 'Can you see anything?' And the man looked up and said, 'I can see people, but they look like trees, walking.' Then Jesus laid his hands on his eyes again; and he looked intently and his sight was restored and he saw everything clearly.[8]

We consider time in a linear way – divided into days, hours, minutes and seconds that can be counted and recorded. Time is a cake with a limited number of slices; when all are accounted for there is no more to eat. We often don't have enough of this 'time' to satisfy all those who want a piece of it. And yet, for all that there were crowds around Jesus, he never seems to have been hurried. When a blind man came there was time to take him by the hand and walk with him out of the village. The encounter needed room – it could not be rushed. How long did the two of them stay together? Were the disciples counting, worrying about what else was on the agenda? When the once-blind man grew older and recalled the day his life changed, it would not have made sense to define the meeting in hours or minutes. Time is more elastic than we imagine. The attention he received was without boundary, even reaching into his present.

For Jesus time was a shelter he was able to offer people; time was hospitality of the heart. The wonder of Jesus' ministry is not so much how he managed to 'fit it all in' but the attention he gave to each person. At this stage the sense of burden might be beginning to build up for those who seek to follow in his footsteps: not only do we have to complete all the tasks in front of us but each needs our full and complete attention. Prepare to be overwhelmed! But Jesus' attitude towards time was founded on a paradox: the more generously you honour your own being by choosing to use time to shelter in those people and places and activities that refresh your spirit, the more time you have for those who need your shelter. Time is measured by depth, not just length. Moments of true presence can bring about

---

[8] Mark 8.22–25.

more than hours of distracted mental absence. Jesus left the crowds, went for long walks up into the hills, and rested in the homely ease of the house of Martha, Mary and Lazarus. He found shade and shelter in the presence of his Father. Without such choices time becomes the driver, and we the slaves that must do its bidding. From the places of his own shelter, Jesus had liberty to take a blind man by the hand and go with him out of his village. There is time.

Getting practical

And high time you might think! How does any of this help with having too much to do and too little time to do it? I have been the recipient of a number of time management courses and even – in the absence of anyone more fitting – attempted to give them. Practical strategies do make a difference. There is a linear dimension of time that we can work with creatively: days off matter; dividing the waking day into three parts and keeping one free for one's own resourcing and refreshment is a healthy practice; crossing time off in advance in whatever diary you keep and then close guarding it can prevent life becoming swamped by the sheer volume of self-generating tasks. There is more advice, and better advice, available and it is good to avail oneself of it. But beyond managing time I believe it also helps to re-imagine how we conceive time and our attitude towards it. In being open to the hospitality of people and places for the sake of our own resourcing, we discover that time also has a depth-dimension. We become more hospitable people: less bullied by the relentless drive of hours and minutes. We won't be rushed in those moments when stillness and presence alone can bring healing.

Let's go elsewhere

In the morning, while it was still very dark, he got up and went out to a deserted place, and there he prayed. And Simon and his companions hunted for him. When they found him they said to him, 'Everyone is searching for you.' He answered, 'Let us go on to the neighbouring towns, so that I may proclaim the message there also, for that is what I came out to do.'[9]

---

[9] Mark 1.35–38.

All of us might have felt hunted down at some point. The needs other people bring to us, or the demands we place on ourselves, come relentlessly in packs to seek us out and pin us to their will. What does Jesus do? He goes missing. And then, when he is found, he goes elsewhere. The respect Jesus shows to his own needs, and his ability to hold on to the larger picture of what belongs to him to do, are closely intertwined. The shelter of place, space and prayer are the source of purpose and of discernment.

Turn over the pages of Mark's Gospel and a different story seems to be told. Seeing the exhaustion of his disciples, Jesus tells them to get in a boat with him and go to the other side of the lake where they can rest. But people guess what they are doing and hurry to where they are going. Looking out on what Jesus had hoped would be 'a deserted place' he sees a 'great crowd' waiting for him. But rather than take flight Jesus 'had compassion for them, because they were like sheep without a shepherd; and he began to teach them many things'.[10] Interruptions happen; plans fall apart; timetables crumble. But rather than succumb to the driver of being the answer to every need – and being that answer *now* – Jesus has the inner space that allows his response to be a free one, moved by compassion. He can be flexible without losing hold of himself or his purpose. When the crowd are fed with word and bread he sends them away, goes back up into the mountains to pray and tells his disciples to get back in the boat, sail across the lake and get some space.[11] In the end all need their shelter. Without it we become scattered sheep, lost and lacking good pasture.

Before you move on, stop to consider these questions:

- Who are my shelters?
- Where are my shelters?
- When do I find shelter?
- What more might I do to receive the rest and refreshment God desires to give me?

---

[10] Mark 6.30–34.
[11] Mark 6.45–46.

A human being, open to God

'Simon, Simon, listen! Satan has demanded to sift all of you like wheat, but I have prayed for you that your own faith may not fail; and you, when once you have turned back, strengthen your brothers.'[12]

A priest shared with me her belief that a priest has to be willing to die in the first years of their ministry. Ordination provides no immunity from human weakness; if anything its demands expose more immediately whatever flaws we carry. Whatever notions we have of superhuman spiritual strength are likely to be swiftly undermined by events: we wade into a situation requiring the most sensitive of interventions with oversized feet; we lose our temper in the face of unreasonable demands; we recognize we are way out of our depth and have no idea how to find dry land. And yet these deaths can also become a new birth: we learn to lean on God rather than any idealized vision of our perfection. In opening ourselves to the compassion of Christ and the grace of the Spirit our true humanity begins to emerge: weak and yet strong; flawed but sometimes beautiful; often self-centred yet capable of astounding generosity. This was the story of Simon the fisherman.

Jesus called Simon 'The Rock' – but what did he mean? Perhaps in those first years of following Jesus, Simon assumed that his master had judged him unshakeable. He was only too willing to believe it. His was the solidity of being right, having control of the situation and standing above the weakness that would lead him to be ruled by fear. But this idealized self-portrait soon crumbled. All the Gospel writers describe the pain of Simon's fall. He was the one who knew better than Jesus what was good for him, only to be told he was the mouthpiece of Satan. He alone got out of the boat but then foundered amid the waves. He asserted how impossible it would be for him to abandon Jesus before denying he ever knew him in the sweat of his fear. He it was who was cast to the ground, broken and weeping, while those women who followed Jesus dared to stand with him at the foot of the cross. And yet it was from these experiences – rather

---

12 Luke 22.31–32.

than despite them – that he became the one to strengthen others. The faith that grew in Simon Peter was not the unwavering certainty of those who have never failed. His faith was in the unwavering compassion of Jesus, who forgave his sins and did not withdraw his trust. What marks Simon the Rock out – and commends him to us – is his courage in turning back to face that compassionate gaze. When Jesus appeared once more on the beach where Simon had first heard his call, he did not hesitate to rush to him through the waves. And when breakfast was finished and Jesus drew him aside, he faced the pain of Jesus' threefold question, 'Do you love me?' when everything in him wanted to turn away. Simon Peter died, to live again in the love of him who called once more: 'Follow me.'[13] The rock on which the Church was founded was not perfection, strength or mastery but the undying capacity to turn afresh to face the compassionate gaze of God in weakness and in sin. The rock on which the Church is built is the daring to trust – despite feelings – that one is yet worthy of being loved. The rock on which the Church is built is the outpouring of this same compassion.

A priest ministers absolution: the release of the heavy weight of wrongdoing and the outpouring of the Spirit who draws us deeper into God's life. Forgiveness is at the heart of Christian life, and it begins with our receiving it. Every priest is a 'Simon' learning to be 'Peter' through their openness to be forgiven and made whole. I have already suggested that rather than speak of modelling the perfection of Christ, with all the danger that has of projecting a self-made 'holiness' that majors on authority but lacks love, it is more helpful to think of a priest as one who seeks to model what it is to be a human being open to God, through the grace of Christ and the communion of the Spirit. Within that openness to God, a priest will experience the sifting of chaff from wheat, for without this there will be no bread to share. Even under the compassionate gaze of God, owning our need of forgiveness and healing is not easy. Yet Jesus continues to pray for his followers, that their faith may not fail. Through the grace of God at work within their weakness, they will go on to strengthen their brothers and sisters.

---

[13] John 21.1–19.

> When it was evening on that day, the first day of the week, and the doors of the house where the disciples had met were locked for fear of the Jews, Jesus came and stood among them and said, 'Peace be with you'. After he said this, he showed them his hands and his side ... Jesus said to them again, 'Peace be with you. As the Father has sent me, so I send you.' When he had said this, he breathed on them and said to them, 'Receive the Holy Spirit. If you forgive the sins of any, they are forgiven them; if you retain the sins of any, they are retained.'[14]

For Jesus, the gift of peace, the breath of the Spirit and the forgiveness of sins belong together. The greeting of peace reaches into the disciples' anxiety, hurt, loss and fear. Though they have separated themselves off, the doors they have closed do not exist for Jesus; he is in their midst; he comes with no desire to burden or blame. He is peace and he gives peace. The breath of the Spirit is the breath of this peace; the life that flows through the disciples in this breathing is forgiveness. For this they are sent.

The doors are closed and yet Jesus stands among them. The story of the Fall in Genesis suggests that disobedience and pride have created a barrier between humankind and God. The Garden of Eden is lost; the tree of life is guarded with a flaming sword lest anyone try to reach it. But for Jesus there is no separation. When Simon Peter tells Jesus to go away from him because he is a sinner, Jesus remains right there.[15] Forgiveness – in God's view – is not as we imagine. There is no account to clear, for God does not count. God goes on beholding us with a love that is not measured or bound with conditions. Forgiveness is the restoration of relationship (or that relationship becoming real for the first time) through our turning to God, whose face is always turned to us. What of amendment of life? Forgiveness does involve a process of conversion. The breath of the Spirit will draw us out of fear and narrowness of heart if we are willing to go on cooperating with its movement. Those to whom peace is

---

[14] John 20.19–23.
[15] Luke 5.1–11.

spoken must choose to align their lives with the outflow of this peace in their relationships with others. Peace is spoken, the Spirit is breathed and the disciples are sent. Peace comes, as Gerard Manley Hopkins wrote, 'with work to do'.[16]

I think it important that priests reflect on the nature of the forgiveness of God they are called to proclaim. Within a process of revitalizing understanding of the sacraments of the Church in the Catholic tradition, focus shifted from 'confession' to 'reconciliation'. 'Confession' places weight on what we do. 'Reconciliation' helps us look into the face of God, who beholds us in love, and into the faces of those whose lives we have touched and will touch. Reconciliation is not about measuring perfection or imperfection; it concerns relationship with others. Whether we consider reconciliation a sacrament or a sacramental rite, it is a beautiful movement of God into human lives. We are turning towards a God of such large love in the recognition that our love is so small. Sometimes when I sat in the 'confessional' on a Saturday morning I wanted to break the walls down, not just because I felt claustrophobic but because I could not believe in the God some oppressed people lived in fear of: a God who minutely measures our shortcomings and takes careful account of our faults. Such exchanges shrink God down to the extremes of our narrowness rather than expand our hearts to experience and express the height, depth, length and breadth of the love of God. Sorrow for harm done and the desire to change direction can be driven by fear or moved by love; the two might outwardly look the same but their effects are very different. One keeps us bound; the other sets us free. One leads us deeper into the mire of seeking self-made perfection; the other moves us to rely on the Spirit's help in our continued weakness. One provides momentary relief from inner accusers; the other draws us to 'do justice, and to love kindness and to walk humbly with God'.[17]

---

[16] 'Peace', in *The Poems of Gerard Manley Hopkins*, 4th edn, revised and enlarged, 1967, edited by W. H. Gardner and N. H. MacKenzie, Oxford: Oxford University Press.

[17] Micah 6.6–8.

Being reconciled

> If anyone is in Christ, there is a new creation: everything old has passed away; see, everything has become new! All this is from God, who reconciled us to himself through Christ, and has given us the ministry of reconciliation; that is, in Christ God was reconciling the world to himself, not counting their trespasses against them, and entrusting the message of reconciliation to us.[18]

When we say, 'I am only human', we are usually seeking to excuse our behaviour and declare the fixed limits of our capacity for change. But this humanity is God's chosen place of dwelling and reconciliation. For anyone in Christ there is a new creation. The reconciliation Paul speaks of is in one sense already complete: there is no separation between humankind and God; no wrongdoing can undo God's choice in Christ to be in us, with us and for us. In another sense reconciliation and new creation are barely begun processes: we are lifelong works of God's love. There remains much in each of us to be disentangled, made whole and set free. To be a minister of reconciliation is to embrace this reality in oneself and for others.

The process of reconciliation mends broken relationships. We use the term when speaking of the work of bringing together groups of people estranged from one another through their differences, the harm of history and the projections of fear. When long-term relationships between individuals break down a third party may be brought in to enable hurts to be aired, misunderstandings to be rectified and agreement about a way ahead to be reached. Paul's 'new creation' works into every dimension of our relationships. We are estranged from who God is. We live uneasily with our neighbours and they with us. We are not comfortable with who we are and who we have been: the conflicts that rage within us; the pain of the harm we have done. Christ comes to reconcile us to God, our neighbour and ourselves. We know from our experience that there is no quick fix, but for anyone who is in Christ there is movement. The sacramental rites of reconciliation enable us to go with this flow of God's patient working. The public confession we make within the Eucharist of our

---

[18] 2 Corinthians 5.17–19.

need for forgiveness and our desire to amend expresses our willingness to cooperate with God in the new creation of our relationships. We cannot offer what we are not open to receive. Priests have to consent daily to God's work of reconciliation.

Julian of Norwich saw contrition, compassion and longing for God as medicines for the soul. Contrition is the willingness to face our wounds, 'nakedly and truthfully'. When we look at God we meet compassion, for what God sees is our sorrow and pain; and these wounds for God are not a cause of shame or blame but 'honours'. These wounds are his wounds. For Julian, compassion for the wounded Christ on the cross is the source of compassion for all those who struggle and hurt, including our suffering selves. Longing for God carries us beyond the dead ends of introspection into cooperation with the work of the Spirit, for though 'we are not always in peace and in love', peace and love 'are always in us, living and working'.[19] Looking back at my time as a priest, I see that anything I was able to say or be for others came from this source of God's ongoing work of reconciliation in my own life. What other source of hope could I share than the one that reached out to touch and heal my own broken relationships with God, self and neighbour? As Jesus said to Simon the Pharisee, 'the one to whom little is forgiven, loves little'.[20]

For most priests there will be particular areas where the need for reconciliation is keenly felt. For one, it might be their relationship with God. Many times I have taken God for granted. I have sometimes blamed God for ills of my own making or the difficulties that come in the ordinary course of life. I have not always bothered to seek God with heart, soul and mind despite all the kindness shown me. My life so far has been a slow soaking of God's humility, generosity and compassion into my fearful, unbelieving spirit. For all of us in our different ways reconciliation takes place as we go on meeting face to face.

Becoming as open and attentive to God as God is to us begins to shape the ways we relate to our – sometimes difficult – neighbours.

---

[19] *Julian of Norwich, Showings*, 1978, translated from the critical text with an introduction by Edmund College and James Walsh, The Classics of Western Spirituality, New Jersey: Paulist Press, chapter 39 (Long Text).
[20] Luke 7.47.

There are particular people we may have issues with, past or present. There are those who have willingly or unintentionally harmed us, leaving us bruised, and undermining our confidence in ourselves or capacity to trust others. There are those we have wronged. There are some whose very presence or way of being draws out the barbed wire in us; we want to shut them out or shoot them down. Reconciliation with our neighbours is inseparable with the work of reconciliation with ourselves. All the time we try and pull out the splinters in our neighbour's eyes we are impaired by the planks of wood in our own. How do we ever put wrongs right? How do we – who espouse to be physicians – cure our own sickness? We can't. This draws us back to God. In laying bare the struggles we carry, we begin to sense what belongs to us to do, and what hidden and deep work belongs to God alone. And all the while God goes on loving us and inviting our trust and cooperation in the work of reconciliation we are involved in together. In one moment we are to let go: to release our desire to punish or blame the other, or to give God the room to go on untangling the complexity of the fears that drive us. In another moment we are invited to step out: to tell our neighbour openly of the difficulty we have with their behaviour, or to show generosity to one who as yet shows none to us.

We live in intolerant times. People choose their camps and demonize those who do not follow their causes, beliefs or way of life. Where does it all come from and how will it end? Etty Hillesum, a Jew living in Amsterdam amid growing Nazi oppression, described her own inner life as a battlefield. The problems of the world have to rest somewhere, she believed, so why not in her? The answer to hatred, division and war on a global scale can never rest entirely on government initiatives or negotiated ceasefires. We have to begin with ourselves:

> All disasters stem from us. Why is there a war? Perhaps because now and then I might be inclined to snap at my neighbour. Because I and my neighbour and everyone else do not have enough love. Yet we could fight war and all its excrescences by

releasing each day the love that is shackled inside and giving it a chance to live.[21]

A divided world where many are hurting needs ministers of reconciliation: people prepared to struggle for peace, and to begin with themselves. Amid the muddle – and even the mess – of our relationships, God is reconciling the world to himself. Can you see it? Everything is becoming new. Will you be part of it?

Colloquy

> The colloquy is made by speaking exactly as one friend speaks to another, or as a servant speaks to his master, now asking him for a favour, now blaming himself for some misdeed, now making known his affairs to him, and seeking advice in them.[22]

Throughout the *Spiritual Exercises* Ignatius Loyola encourages the practice of 'colloquy'. For him a colloquy is an intimate conversation, where heart meets heart and truth meets truth. There is neither need nor place for tidying away what is messy or avoiding what is uncomfortable or unresolved. This is a step away from the conversational prayer advocated in my youth, where formality was the order of the day and actual feelings were to be held in check in favour of fixed responses of praise, thanksgiving or contrition. This is the talk of friend with friend, without need for small talk. Lest we forget whom we address, Ignatius also frames the conversation as between servant and master; but this master is also servant, and names us as friends. The details of our lives matter here: there is room to share our experience and its impact on us; to own our need of forgiveness and healing; to ask for guidance and to seek help.

Some ways of prayer face us with the transcendence of God. We leave behind words and concepts in favour of attentive receptiveness. Without denying this transcendence, the prayer of colloquy draws us into the mystery of God's intimacy. As in so many scenes in the

---

[21] Etty Hillesum, 1999, A*n Interrupted Life: The Diaries and Letters of Etty Hillesum 1941–1943*, London: Persephone Books, p. 116.
[22] Louis J. Puhl SJ, 1951, *The Spiritual Exercises of St. Ignatius: Based on studies in the language of the autograph*, Chicago: Loyola University Press. Exx 54.

Gospels, no one else is there. Jesus has drawn us away from the crowd. He walks with us along the road or sits by our side. I ask myself: 'Why am I important? Why does he turn to me?' This familiarity is beyond fathoming.

Ignatius places colloquy towards the end of specific prayer exercises. Contemplation leads into relationship and reconciliation. We are opening the particular stirrings of this day to the larger movement of God's wholeness into our brokenness, and then through us into the world. Colloquy is not only for unburdening, it is also for transformation. As well as words to share there are words to hear. There will be spaces between words that are full of communication.

Etty Hillesum's journal began as way of getting out her thoughts and feelings and reflecting on their significance. But more and more it became a colloquy:

> I am beginning to feel a little more peaceful, God, thanks to this conversation with You. You are sure to go through lean times with me now and then, when my faith weakens ... but, believe me, I shall always labour for You ... and I shall never drive You from my presence.[23]

Writing may become your own way of reviewing your experience in the intimate company of God. As you go on you may begin to sense you are not alone in shaping the words that flow.

How do we enter into this conversation of friend with friend and servant with master? With the unstrained ease of those who know their company is welcomed. When do we pray this way? Often: when there is something important to say; when we need the company of one who understands us better than we do ourselves; when we are hurting or rejoicing; when we want to know what to do or how to be; as much as friends will when they have opportunity to share their lives.

---

[23] Hillesum, p. 218.

7

A Rule of Life for Priests?

Do not neglect the gift that is in you, which was given to you through prophecy with the laying on of hands by the council of elders. Put these things into practice, devote yourself to them, so that all may see your progress.[1]

I have suggested that the spiritual life of many priests suffers for lack of the support structures provided by a religious congregation: a common rule of life and a community to whom one is accountable for its observance. In the absence of these, priests have the liberty to work out their own ways of serving those in their care while remaining open to God and looking after their own welfare. However, the expectations attached to priesthood are so great that the good intentions of many priests are simply swept away. Some – through no fault of their own – have never fully grasped the importance of respecting their own human needs. Others have not yet developed the deep roots in God that allow them to find genuine rest, refreshment and resilience in the face of the challenges that come. As a priest I floundered in these areas and often felt isolated. It's sink or swim, and in those circumstances most priests will find ways to get by, but often without flourishing.

I have also suggested that the varied contexts within which priests work – along with differences in personality – pose significant obstacles against creating a detailed pattern of observance that is relevant and helpful for all. However, many dispersed communities (such as the Third Order of the Society of St. Francis or the Community of Aidan and Hilda) face similar challenges. Their members come from all walks of life. Some work full time and have care of children, while

---

[1] 1 Timothy 4.14–15.

others are retired. The rule of life they adopt works flexibly, taking account of their different needs. There are shared lines of orientation: attitudes and values to live by, and practices that members commit to. Even though people live apart and have varied demands on their time, they will meet now and then to pray and share with one another and renew their commitment. Commonly they will receive help in adapting the community's rule of life to their own circumstances; they will also have to account in some way for their observance of it. Might a similar approach work for priests?

As I have expressed, one way of seeking a more sustaining way of life as a priest might be to join such an existing dispersed community. Not everyone will want to do this, or find there is a pattern of commitment that works with their role as a priest or particular personality. But the need for support structures, community and accountability remain if a sustaining form of spiritual life is to be maintained. Should you doubt the need of it, step outside the world of the Church and the same patterns are repeated. Those who succeed in changing the pattern of their lives through Twelve Step programmes come to realize that the disciplines they adopt are necessary for their wellbeing and must be continued beyond any immediate crisis. We could attempt to learn a new language on our own but our efforts are more likely to be sustained if we go to a class, get homework and are encouraged to speak out despite our mistakes and mispronunciations. It is possible to lose weight as an individual but many find it easier when they belong to a group where there is a sense of shared endeavour, recommended practice and mutual accountability. The frameworks adopted are never the end in themselves, but without them the desired goal can remain elusive.

In what follows I will give some examples of what a rule of life for a priest might look like, and provide some principles for forming your own. But given the sometimes well-founded resistance or suspicion many of us have towards imposed structures or observances I want not only to examine the 'rule' but the place of the will in deciding to live by it.

Where there's a will there's a way

The language of 'rule' is problematic for many people. Sometimes rules serve the interests of those who set them, rather than those who must observe them. A 'rule of life' might suggest the imposition of one person's will upon another. Such rules are there to be ignored, broken or overthrown when the opportunity occurs. Jesus criticized those who sought compliance to the rule of tithing mint, cumin and dill while neglecting the spirit of justice, mercy and faith that underpinned the Law.[2] Though Jesus gave commands – not least to love the neighbour and forgive their wrongdoing – the underlying response he sought in those he challenged was always a freely given one. Life is there as a gift to be chosen. Jesus himself declared that though he laid down his life, no one took it from him.[3]

More than rules, Jesus talked about paths. There is a way to be walked: 'Follow me.' The first name of the Christian community – 'The Way' – suggests this alignment of practice with freedom. Here is a distinctive and purposeful pattern of life, and here is the choice you are invited to make to go with it. The will is placed at the very centre of discipleship. Go where your heart leads you. To say 'your will be done' with Jesus is to do so from a place of liberty and generosity. Even when the path is difficult it remains one to be chosen out of love rather than observed out of fear and subservience.

It might help, then, to speak about choosing to follow a *way* of life, rather than observe a *rule* of life. In so doing we are setting ourselves to move purposefully towards goals we have chosen – but where are we moving? The first answers might flow from our own assessment of what we need for our own flourishing and the effectiveness of our ministry: perhaps I recognize the need for a firmer practice of prayer, or to make more time for the important people in my life. The deeper questions to which we seek answers are relational ones: What will it take for me to move further into God? What is required for God to become my mover?

Properly understood, the language of 'rule' can also be helpful. The origin of the term lies in the Latin *regula*, meaning a measure or a

---

2 Matthew 23.23–24.
3 John 10.17–18.

means of finding direction. We might choose a rule because we need to measure out our time with more consideration, or to help guide us when we are disorientated. Knowing ourselves, we might realize that our good intentions are not enough; we need to make our own rules to safeguard what we know works for our wellbeing. As the psalmist knows, 'rule' and 'way' can inform one another:

> Lead me in the path of your commandments,
> for I delight in it ...
> I shall walk at liberty,
> for I have sought your precepts.[4]

A way is expressed in purposeful steps – chosen rather than imposed. A rule can liberate us from all that drives us when it moves us into the freedom of God.

Towards a way of life

> He [the abbot]) must so arrange everything that the strong have something to yearn for and the weak have nothing to run from.[5]

A rule of life is not an end in itself. Neither is it meant to be harsh or burdensome. It must be related to your particular context and constraints. However, to be meaningful it will have a sense of challenge: it is intended to safeguard adequate time for those activities you recognize to be essential for your growth but that in practice may not yet be established as part of your routine. As Benedict in his wisdom suggests, let what you decide to do take you further in the direction you yearn for, and let it also be realistic and achievable. Otherwise you will quickly give up.

Below I will list some areas of spiritual life related to priestly ministry, drawing on the section headings in the Rain for Roots chapters of this book. I will also make some tentative suggestions for practices that might support your growth; some recur more than once. *You won't do everything*; it wouldn't be helpful to you or anyone else to try and do so. As you read through – and as you reflect on your life – ask God to show you where to begin. Is it with making space in

---

[4] Psalm 119.35, 45.
[5] *The Rule of St Benedict*, Chapter 64.

your day to notice what is taking place in your inward and outward worlds? Or perhaps you recognize the need to take more care in looking after yourself through rest and recreation? Having identified an area, spend some time prayerfully reflecting on what might make a difference to your life. Be realistic, not demanding more of yourself than you can deliver, but at the same time be bold. It may also help to think about your life within different timeframes. Consider what you will build into:

- each day
- each week
- each month
- each year.

You will find more detailed guidance on these practices and ways of prayer in the relevant chapters.

To be with him

Discipleship has its source in actively choosing to be in Jesus' company. You are called to this intimacy. Jesus invites you to make your home in him as he makes his home in you. Fruitfulness in ministry rests in this mutual abiding. Find pauses and spaces within your day, week, month and year to be present to God's presence with you.

- Make a physical place of prayer in your home. Set aside some space that has this purpose, and this purpose alone. Place within it whatever helps you settle into the presence of God – a candle, images, a Bible or an icon.
- You are always on holy ground. Spend five minutes each day being present to what is around you through your senses.
- Decide on a time in your day that you can regularly give to being present to God. Be practical and realistic in your thinking: How long will you set aside? Where will you go? What might get in the way of your good intention and what can you do about this? If at all possible leave your phone behind or switch it off.
- Each year set aside some time away from the parish to go on retreat. Arrange this at an early stage so that commitments that come in do not crowd this out.

- Each month go to a quiet place for a morning or a day where you can reflect, read and pray without the disturbance of work.

Dwelling with the Word

The word of God is spoken within the Scriptures and through the events of daily life. As a priest you are called to listen, look and be aware. You pour into the mixing bowl of contemplative openness to God's presence the words of the Bible and the movements in your own life and in the lives of those you serve. Here is where the bread of life is formed and then shared.

- Spend time daily on praying with Scripture through *lectio divina*. Give room to allow rain from these words to soak down to your roots. You may also find other spiritual reading helpful. Approach this in the same way, paying attention to particular passages or sentences that seem to be for you. An online resource such as *Pray as you go* may also be useful.[6]
- Take a walk each week through part of your parish. Here too the word of God is being spoken. What do you notice? It might help to imagine Jesus walking with you. Pray for the people and places you pass. When you have finished your walk spend a few minutes reflecting on what you have seen.

The priest as pilgrim traveller

You are a priest and a traveller, and you guide a pilgrim people. The faith you profess and live by does not consist of settled certainties but the risk of trust in following one who calls you beyond what you know. Your vocation goes on unfolding. Your church's mission within its neighbourhood continues to develop. Tools of discernment will help you sense the invitation of the Spirit and appropriate ways of responding.

- Make the *examen* part of your daily practice of prayer. Rather than rush through it, set outside 15 minutes that are for this alone.

---

[6] www.pathwaystogod.org.

- If you have a spiritual director, review how helpful this relationship is. Are there further ways they might be able to help you? Is it time to seek someone new? If you lack a spiritual director at this time make it a priority to find one who can accompany, encourage and challenge you.
- Make a daily walk part of your life. Allow the rhythm of your footsteps to slow you down, so that you can be alive to what is around you, and present to God who goes with you.
- In this coming year make a walking pilgrimage to a place that holds spiritual significance for you.
- Consider the setting up of an annual pilgrimage day / morning for your parish.

The priest as servant

As a priest you have power. Reflect on the power you have; own it for the gift and the burden it is. Christ our Lord is also Christ our servant. Humility helps us use power creatively in the service of others. A servant is also a 'waiter' – one who knows that the work they are engaged in and the food they share is not their own. Rather than attempt to 'lord it over' other people or the course of events, the priest as servant is challenged to be open to their mystery. They take hold of responsibility, but also let it go to God.

- Use the practice of a daily *examen* to deepen your self-awareness and help you move beyond self-obsession.
- As you begin a new day take hold of what you are responsible for, and then let it go to God.
- Build up the habit of taking small pauses between activities to rest and be refreshed. This is time to put down your bowl of water and towel and let Jesus wash your tired feet.

Minister of communion

We are made in the image and likeness of God, whose life is communion. This mutuality of giving and receiving is expressed each time we celebrate the Eucharist. We are one body in Christ, dependent on one another for our wholeness and growth. Priests are not only ministers of communion but participants in it; they too need to be nurtured, encouraged and understood.

- Each day, or each week, share a time of open prayer, silence or part of the daily Office with others. Take turns in leading this.
- If and when you have opportunity, instead of presiding at the Eucharist take your place as part of the congregation.
- Consider joining a dispersed Christian community with opportunities for fellowship and the support of a shared rule of life.
- Explore with friends – clergy or lay – whether you might meet once a month to eat, share and pray together.

Celebrant of the Incarnation

Through their ministry priests proclaim that all that has being is the word of God made flesh. We are people of the body and physical movements express the inner workings of our spirit. Liturgy uses what we can touch, taste, hear, smell and see to invite us more deeply into God. Sometimes, when we have no words, the body can lead us into prayer. We are called to respect and honour our physical being, for it houses God.

- Make space each day / each week for a physical activity that refreshes your spirit: carving wood, making bread, taking a walk, working in the garden, or going for a run.
- Consider whether you get enough physical rest. If not, what change might you make?
- Reflect on how well you eat. Do you allow enough time to prepare food that is balanced and nourishing? If you regularly eat food while you continue working consider how you might step away from your commitments and find physical space and time to eat, even if this is limited in duration. Switch off your phone!
- If you struggle to find the inner stillness and receptiveness of prayer, reflect on what physical activity helps you relax: this is where you might find a resting place with God. Each day / each week, enjoy time spent in this way and invite God to share it with you.

The herald of good news

The ministry of priests is one of hope. God is in our broken world and working purposefully to renew it. In each one of us a new gospel is being written. God is creating anew, once more coming alongside, turning our deaths into fresh resurrections and drawing us from division into interdependence. The kingdom is in our midst and we are invited to be heralds of its awakening.

- As part of your daily *examen* give thanks to God for all the gifts of the day.
- Make regular use of a journal to record the different ways you experience God's good news in your life.
- Each year spend a day retracing the working of God through your life. Remembering the past will help you be more alive to the flow of the Spirit within your life in the present.

With your own place to shelter

We all need a shelter from the rainstorm and shade from the heat. Friends, partners and children can help us step out of the expectations that come with being a priest, and enable us to recover our sense of being a person first and last. Visits to familiar places can help us settle into a different inner space where we can genuinely begin to unwind, find refreshment and experience the hospitality of God. Time often feels our enemy, but it can also be our friend if we honour our own needs and set aside hours that belong to us alone.

- Each day set aside some quality time for your partner and your children. It might be more limited on some days than others, but don't allow it to be regularly squeezed out.
- Set aside a regular time each week that is just for you, your partner and / or your children where there is enough space to get away from the workplace and enjoy being with one another.
- Each month plan an outing or a treat of some kind with those who are closest to you.
- Each month spend at least part of a day with a friend who radiates life to you.
- Meet each month with a spiritual director or mentor.

- Review how you spend your allotted time off. Is it time off? Resolve to make it so, rather than using it to squeeze in those extra commitments that don't fit into your week's work.
- Use a shed or a corner of your home to make a physical prayer space.
- Spend a day a month / every two months at a local retreat house where you can find time apart to rest, reflect and pray.
- Each week go to a place where you feel refreshed and renewed. It might be a park, an art gallery, the seaside or a music venue.

A human being, open to God

A priest models what it is to be a human being open to the grace of God operating through weakness. As ministers of forgiveness and healing, priests also need to be restored and made whole. Like anyone else, they will find some relationships difficult; they will not always feel equal to the tasks set before them. God goes on reconciling the world to himself through Christ; all stand in need of this reconciliation. Contrition, compassion and longing for God keep us open to receive and share the healing of love.

- Use a daily *examen* to recognize, own and release to God your need of healing and forgiveness.
- Spend some time each day before a cross or crucifix. Lay down any burden you carry before Christ. It may help to do this physically: for example, by holding stones in your hand and then putting them down by the cross.

Moving step by step along the way

If you have moved through this checklist you may well have come up with a number of changes you want to make to the pattern of your life and prayer. Realistically you will struggle to do everything at once. It is often more effective to concentrate initially on one or two areas and move them safely from aspiration to reality rather than expect yourself to reshape your entire life overnight. It is likely that you will experience difficulty in making a change; you will be moving against patterns of being and working that have become established over time. Your default responses will sometimes defeat you. Expect this to happen, but rather than give up at this point, renew your commitment. If you recognize you have taken too large a bite, draw in your expectations to what is achievable. But be careful! Don't give everything away because it proves difficult. New patterns take consistent effort and deliberate intention before they become part of what you naturally do. It will get easier. Once you have consolidated some initial steps, you can begin to move on to others. Rather than a means of instant transformation, the rule of life you aspire to is a pattern to grow into gradually.

In forming and moving into a new rule of life it is useful – perhaps vital – to have a mentor or spiritual director who can work with you through all stages of the process. They provide a chosen place of accountability for this journey you are making. They can help clarify what your deepest needs are and explore practical means of addressing them. If you attempt to take on more than is achievable they can help draw you back to what is realistic. If you slip away from the commitments you have made they may gently challenge you and help you explore what has got in the way of your chosen path. What they will not do is impose a predetermined plan for the ways your life and prayer are to be shaped. Whatever you decide on and aim to live by is between you and God. The role of your spiritual director is to support you in discerning the movement of the Spirit in your life and identifying those practical steps that will help you cooperate with this flow.

There may be other people whose input is helpful in this process. You may find it beneficial to share your intentions with a close friend, regular prayer companion or your partner. They will be on your side (and sometimes on your case) if and when you abandon your desired new steps. It may be helpful for them to understand what changes you are making and why, so that they can work with you rather than against you. If you are going to make a real effort not to be involved in any work on your day off, or to be unavailable at certain times, it might help to tell people in the congregation that this is the case. Some will ignore the message, but many will want to support you in this.

A rule of life is an expression of conversion, a practical means of resolving to follow Christ and to be transformed through the journey; the 'rule' is also a 'way'. For this reason it can never be set in stone. The Spirit is the primary mover: we hear its sound but we do not know where it comes from or where it goes. We are asked to remain flexible and receptive as new needs and opportunities emerge. Together, priest and spiritual director set themselves to listen afresh to the Spirit. What practical response is now invited? What is the next step along the way?

8

What Can We Do to Support the Spiritual Life of Priests?

> Speaking the truth in love, we must grow up in every way into him who is the head, into Christ, from whom the whole body, joined and knitted together by every ligament with which it is equipped, as each part is working properly, promotes the body's growth in building itself up in love.[1]

We are responsible one for another. The growth of the body rests on each member's flourishing. The welfare and spiritual health of priests rests in part on those charged with their initial training and ongoing formation. As much as priests are formed to be carers, they must also be readied to take responsibility for their own wellbeing, and to allow others to care for them. Those who make appointments and supervise ministry face the continual challenge of listening to the experience of priests on the ground and responding with creativity to their needs. While priests serve the people of their parish, congregation members are also called to look after their priests.

Diocesan structures, programmes of initial and ongoing formation, and local church dynamics vary widely from place to place, and so the recommendations I will make will be general rather than detailed. Recent years have seen a number of different initiatives aimed at resourcing the life and ministry of priests. I do not attempt to survey these or comment on their effectiveness. These thoughts emerge from my contact with priests and reflection on my own experience.

---

[1] Ephesians 4.15–16.

Discernment of a rule of life, supported by a spiritual director or mentor

My sense is that the pressures on priests are such that without a well considered and consistently applied rule of life the quality of their spiritual life and general wellbeing will suffer. As I have suggested earlier, a rule of life appropriate for priests is fitted to the individual rather than being uniform, and chosen rather than externally imposed. It will evolve over time rather than be fixed. While it will focus on ensuring a steady supply of rain to sustain and refresh the spiritual life of a priest, it will also embrace practical provision for their overall physical, emotional and social flourishing.

The role of a spiritual director and mentor in helping to draw up, monitor and revise the rule of life is vital. Their task is to accompany rather than direct. Together, priest and spiritual director will spend time discerning what specific needs are and what might work in practice. A framework such as the one I have provided may be helpful. The rule is not an end in itself but a means of responding to the Spirit's invitation to live the fullness of our individual being generously through the deepening of our relationship with God. As situations change and as growth takes place both priest and director will need to be alive to the Spirit's leading. The rule is also a way; it provides stability but also supports movement. What worked in the first few years of ordained ministry may not be the same 20 years on. While a spiritual director provides an agreed – rather than enforced – place of accountability for personal and spiritual wellbeing, they are no part of any external assessment. Their sole role is to support the priest in remaining open to the Spirit.

Given that many priests feel the weight of too many expectations, I suggest using the term 'way of life' rather than 'rule of life'. The latter has a long history, and as I have explored, when properly understood is rich in meaning. But 'way' avoids connotations of conformity and burden; it also reinforces how all priests are on an adventure of discipleship, responding to the call of one who says: 'Follow me.'

The role of a spiritual director goes beyond helping the priest they accompany to discern a way of life. They are there for the long term as supporter, encourager and reference point for the journey into God.

Being outside parish and diocesan structures they provide a safe and free space where truth can be spoken, doubts and frustrations aired, and dreams and longings explored. From the beginning of exploring vocation, through formation, ordination and ministry, a priest needs such a person. I recognize there is often a shortage of trained and skilled spiritual directors. It may be that a diocese puts in place a system of mentors to ensure that at least some support is available. In essence, however, their role is no different from that of spiritual directors, and they will need similar training and supervision.

Supervision

Along with spiritual direction priests need regular supervision. The purposes of the two ministries are closely related but distinct. The focus of a spiritual director lies in enabling those they accompany to become attentive and responsive to the work of the Holy Spirit. A supervisor holds together concern for the ministry exercised by a priest on behalf of the Church with concern for their growth and flourishing. The last thing priests on the ground want is a watchful eye critically observing each and every movement they make; but a lack of supervision can leave priests feeling isolated and unsupported by the Church they serve. In another era, I cannot remember receiving any supervision in my time as a priest. It is important to the spiritual and emotional wellbeing of priests that the Church hears and responds to their experiences and learns from what is shared. Most dioceses will have in place a system of regular ministerial review; those involved in providing this supervision need adequate training and support.

A community of faith

My sense is that every priest would benefit from experiencing themselves as part of a community where prayer can be offered together, truths safely spoken, and support shared. A priest working in a parish setting is already part of a community of faith. However, their role creates limits on the degree of mutuality that can exist. There will be some things that cannot be shared; there will often be an uneven weight of expectations falling more heavily on the side of the priest. Is community for everyone? Some of us are more naturally gregarious than others. I have a strong need for personal space and I have not always found it easy to fit into groups. But I have also come to realize that unless my desire for solitude goes hand in hand with a movement into relationship I am out of tune with the triune God in whose image I am made. We find wholeness in and through one another by the giving and receiving of love. A degree of separation seems written into the practical reality of ministry as a priest; separation can easily become isolation.

What might a community of faith look like? For some it might mean joining an existing dispersed religious community such as the Iona Community or the Third Order of the Society of St Francis. Others may already have a tight-knit group of friends, priests and lay, with whom they meet regularly. Dioceses may encourage setting up small peer groups of priests. Following an initiative set up by my own diocese, I joined up with a small peer group, and after 30 years we still meet up every other month, even though some of us have left the ministry. The answer does not have to be the same for each person. Exploring where and how one finds community can be an integral part of drawing up a way of life with the support of a spiritual director. For the community of faith to be something more than a label, it will need to have some meaningful shape:

- *Meeting regularly:* Monthly, or at least every other month.
- *Eating a meal together:* Sharing food creates bonds of belonging.
- *Allowing time for sharing of experience:* Rather than getting stuck in talking 'shop' there is active encouragement for each person to talk about what really matters – whether this is directly related to ministry or not. Confidentiality is held within the group.
- *Praying together:* Every meeting includes time to be before God together – whether this is in silence, through *lectio divina*, a shared *examen* or in some other form.

There are other ingredients that may prove to be important. The value of 'play' is not to be underestimated. We all end up taking ourselves too seriously and it's good to forget everything for a while and have some fun. It might be helpful to have an annual overnight stay away.

Rain for roots

For water to reach down to roots rain must be sustained. A sudden downpour succeeds in wetting the ground, but much of the water runs away without penetrating the hard crust of the surface. Regular soakings of prayer are needed to reach and sustain depth of spiritual life.

This begins with priestly formation. Time is pressured and academic demands are high; but without generous provision of time for prayer, deep and resilient roots of relationship with God will not form. However thorough programmes of formation are, it serves all involved to remember that the primary role in this endeavour belongs to the Holy Spirit. Only before the 'I AM' of God do we become who we are.

Hours of the Office are often an integral part of college life – whether residential or non-residential. Important as this is, students for the priesthood also need opportunity to befriend silence and solitude and to explore a variety of ways of prayer. This exposure to the possibilities of prayer can help ordinands find practices that can work with who they are and that are capable of sustaining them spiritually in the longer term. I have used the metaphor of 'soaking' and that feels important. A short drizzle of common prayer will not do it. Time, repetition and the active support of a spiritual director are all needful. An annual retreat that is less content led and allows more personal space can also be helpful.

Beyond ordination the need for regular soaking continues. Beyond the personal practice worked out as part of a way of life, I believe it would be helpful for dioceses to promote (or organize) individually guided retreats in support of priests at different stages of ministry: perhaps after three years from ordination and thereafter every seven years. The advantage of an individually guided retreat over a led retreat is that the former has no set agenda but instead starts with where the individual is. With the backdrop of silence and solitude, the daily conversation with a guide allows exploration of whatever arises from the whole life experience of the retreatant. The guide can suggest prayer exercises that work with the personality of the one they accompany and that relate in some way to their context. Other forms of retreat may well turn out to be equally valid and helpful, and the tone adopted by a diocese is more usefully one of encouragement and normalization of the practice rather than external imposition. Many priests are already faithful to the practice of an annual retreat of some form. But beyond allowing the space for priests to take a retreat, dioceses may need to go further in saying, 'This matters ... you matter ... take some time apart for you and God.'

Support within the local church

I began this chapter with an image from the letter to the Ephesians: growth takes place in the body when each part understands they are there for the other. Priests in their humanity need the kinds of support we all do: kindness, thoughtfulness and encouragement. They can be prickly and impatient. They have boundaries that they need to uphold and ask you to respect. Sometimes they need saving from themselves. They will not always accept help readily. Be hospitable without forcing hospitality. Offer help when you see it is needed. Give them space when you sense that is what they need. Listen when they want to let something go and need a place to be heard. Keep sight of the person within the priest. Hold them in your prayer. They are on a journey too; you are disciples together.